3 9100 00569 505 4

DUE DATE

APR 09. 90

OCT 26.

JAN   92

SEP 28. 93

FEB 02.

17. AUG

FEB 2 2

SEP 22.

OCT 28. 95

SINCE THIS BOOK IS
NO LONGER IN DEMAND
TORONTO PUBLIC LIBRARY
IS OFFERING IT FOR SALE.

Toronto
Public
Library

Bits 'n Bytes About Computing:
A Computer Literacy Primer

BOOKS OF INTEREST

Wayne Amsbury
Structured Basic and Beyond

M. Carberry, H. Khalil, J. Leathrum, and L. Levy
Foundations of Computer Science

William Findlay and David Watt, Second Edition
Pascal: An Introduction to Methodical Programming

Rachelle S. Heller and C. Dianne Martin
Bits 'n Bytes About Computing: A Computer Literacy Primer

Harold Lawson
Understanding Computer Systems

David Levy
Chess and Computers

David Levy and Monroe Newborn
More Chess and Computers

Tom Logsdon
Computers and Social Controversy
Computers and Social Controversy Workbook

Ira Pohl and Alan Shaw
The Nature of Computation: An Introduction to Computer Science

Donald D. Spencer
Computers in Number Theory

Bits 'n Bytes
About Computing:
A Computer Literacy Primer

Rachelle S. Heller
University of Maryland
& C. Dianne Martin
University of Maryland

Computer Science Press

020017

Copyright   ©   1982 Computer Science Press, Inc.

Printed in the United States of America.

All rights reserved. No part of this book may be reproduced in any form, including photostat, microfilm, and xerography, and not in information storage and retrieval systems, without permission in writing from the publisher, except by a reviewer who may quote brief passages in a review or as provided in the Copyright Act of 1976.

TORONTO
PUBLIC
LIBRARY

PALMERSTON
BRANCH

Computer Science Press
11 Taft Court
Rockville, MD 20850 U.S.A.

2 3 4 5 6   87 86 85 84 83 82

Library of Congress Cataloging in Publication Data
Heller, Rachelle.
Bits 'n bytes about computing.

   Includes index.
   1. Computers.   2. Electronic data processing.
I. Martin, C. Dianne.   II. Title.   III. Title: Bits 'n bytes.
QA76.H3925 1982   001.64   82-2515
ISBN 0-914894-26-9   AACR2

The working manuscript for this book was prepared on a word-processor. The final version of the text was recorded on magnetic tape and then used as input for a UNIX* system interfaced with a Mergenthaler Linotron 202, which composed the book's pages.

*UNIX is a Trademark of Bell Labs.

Digitized image produced by Tsai-Hong Hong on a PDP-11/45 at the Computer Vision Lab, University of Maryland.
Cover picture courtesy of SOURCE Telecomputing Corp., McLean, Va.

001.64
HEL

SEP 2 6 1983

Contents

Chapter 5

What Do Computers Do for Us? 93

Chapter 6

Where Do We Fit into the Computer Picture? 123

Chapter 7

Preface

BITS 'N BYTES ABOUT COMPUTING was written with the classroom teacher in mind. It is the hope of the authors that this book will fill a real educational need, that of providing information about computers geared to teachers at all levels. The material in this book has already been used successfully in computer literacy workshops for elementary school teachers, and the topics covered are the ones teachers themselves have requested. We believe this book will be a valuable tool for the preservice training of new teachers as well as upgrading the skills of teachers already in the profession.

The activities at the end of each chapter, when done by teachers in a seminar or education methods course, have proven to be sufficient for imparting computer literacy skills. Experience has shown that when teachers do the activities themselves, they gain insight into how these activities could be used in their classrooms. In addition, as the activities are worked through, the teachers produce visual aids for instructional use. Our aim is that this book will become a source of information and activities which classroom teachers will find suitable to adapt to their teaching environments. As teachers become familiar with the material in this book, we hope they will be comfortable choosing among the topics and activities as they integrate computer-related material into their own curriculum.

In the world of computers, a **bit** is the smallest unit of information stored inside of a computer. A **byte** is a larger unit of information made up of a sequence of bits. We have called our book *Bits 'n Bytes* because on some topics we have offered the teacher just a bit of information. On other topics, such as Chapter 4 on problem-solving, we have provided a hearty byte of information.

Each chapter in this book is organized so that the content material is first, followed by a list of key ideas or vocabulary words. These are followed by a set of student activities. Each activity is written from the point of view of the student and is followed by a Teacher's Corner which describes the purpose, materials needed, time involved, skills, follow-up activities and additional information needed for the activity. Some of the activities are intended to be brief classroom activities while others are long term or on-going homework assignments. At the end of each chapter is a list of related readings for teachers and students.

Many people have asked why we chose not to present a programming language in this book. Our feeling is that there are many good books available which teach programming languages. Most teachers have the opportunity, through local adult education programs, to learn "how to program." In addition we did not want to commit this book to a particular programming language. BASIC is probably the most popular language, but there are many different versions. There are also versions of LOGO or Pascal, two other powerful and popular languages, available on the small, personal computers. We chose to limit the scope of this book by not presenting a particular language, in order not to limit the audience which we hope to reach.

Finally, we realize that not every classroom teacher has access to computers in the classroom. The material in this book is not dependent on having a computer! In our opinion it contains all of the information needed by the teacher to become computer literate and can be used in the classroom with or without a computer. Although there is no programming per se, there are many excellent pre-programming activities designed to prepare teachers and their students for the time when they learn programming. In addition we have included, in an appendix, a software evaluation checklist to aid teachers in their examination of educational programs available on computers. We have attempted to include all of the computer awareness topics defined by experts in computer education over the past five years as being essential to meeting the major educational challenge of the 1980's—that of universal computer literacy in our schools.

There are many people who have helped us with this text at various stages in its development. It is impossible to describe what everyone has done. We would simply like to express our gratitude to our colleagues, William Atchison, Richard Austing, and Ben Shneiderman of the University of Maryland, Beverly Hunter and Carol Hargan of HumRRO, Beverly Sangston and Pat Cutlip of Montgomery County Public Schools, Marge Gerrity, Sherry Jacobs, Anne Keister, Sandy Merriam, Judy Glick and Donna Fisher, thirty enthusiastic teachers of the Computer Literacy Summer Workshop of 1981 and the excellent staff at Computer Science Press.

Lastly we must thank our husbands, Steve Heller and Dave Martin, and our children Joshua, Adam and Matthew Heller, and Jennifer and Chuck Martin, without whom this book would have been finished much sooner.

Rachelle S. Heller
C. Dianne Martin
January 1982

Chapter 1

What Is Computer Literacy?

INTRODUCTION

Recently a network newscaster reporting on the INFO '81 Conference commented, *"From the time we are awakened until the time we arrive at our office, the average American comes in contact with at least 50 computerized effects."* Such effects might range from a tiny computer mechanism in a coffee pot to computer controlled traffic lights. This statement is especially amazing when we realize it may only encompass about two hours of a working adult's day. Let us consider the changes that have taken place over the past forty years in just one small area. We will look at the scenario of waking up in the morning.

"As a young child, my mother would come into my room and wake me up in the morning. When I became school aged, I received a wind-up clock to wake me up on school days. Somewhat later I received an electric alarm clock which needed only to be set for the proper hour. For a sixteenth birthday present I received a clock radio. That radio, which awakened me for my college classes, has been replaced by a digital clock radio which not only awakens me, but also starts a pot of coffee. Most recently, I gave my child a solar-powered digital watch which awakens him with a different tune every morning of the week, even playing 'Happy Birthday' on his special day. This watch also provides him with the date and the time, accurate in seconds, for all the time zones around the world, allows him to do numerical calculations and is programmed with a bowling game."

The scenario mirrors the all encompassing changes that have rapidly taken place over the last four decades due to the introduction of computer technology into every area of our lives. We are in the midst of an unparalleled technological revolution with the potential to change the very fabric of our lives.

To date there are over one quarter of a million large and medium scale computers in operation in this country. The small personal computer market is projected to be of equal or greater magnitude. There are several millions of Americans whose job it is to be directly involved with designing, programming and operating computers. Countless others in a variety of occupations use computers as a tool. There are also hundreds of thousands of hobbyists who enjoy the recreational aspects of computers. In fact, computers are so pervasive in our American way of life that we have all become users of and are all affected by computers in some way.

Computer Literacy Defined

In spite of the proliferation of computers throughout our society, there remains a large segment of the population which is computer illiterate. As a result, this lack of knowledge and understanding leads to misconceptions, anxieties and distorted expectations about what computers can be made to do and what they cannot be made to do. It is essential that the growing disparity between the "haves" and "have nots" of computing literacy be addressed. In the context of American society the school classroom is the primary place where **computer literacy** education will most likely occur.

Ten years ago the pioneers in the field of computer-assisted learning predicted that by 1980 all children would have access to computers in their classrooms. Budgetary constraints have prevented most school systems from obtaining large-scale computer equipment needed to reach this goal. However, the advent of low-cost, low-energy **microcomputer** systems is now allowing many schools to obtain computing power. For the past five years leaders in the field of computer education have been calling for universal computer literacy as the major goal for the instructional use of computers in the 1980's.

In addition with the availability of portable microcomputer equipment the whole concept of what constitutes computer literacy has undergone a marked change. In the past, having an awareness and appreciation for computers was sufficient to be computer literate. Now a functional knowledge of computing has been added to the definition. It has been said that computer literacy is "whatever a person needs to know and do with computers in order to function in our information-based society (1) ."

Currently, there is a basic agreement on a number of aspects of computer literacy. Two National Science Foundation (NSF) funded projects, directed toward different areas of the computer impact on society, specify that computer literacy involves a knowledge of the following; (1) how computers work; (2) step-by-step technique for problem solving; (3) social implications; and (4) computer applications. One of the projects included a three day workshop in the summer of 1978 during which approximately 30 persons, principally experts in various areas of the societal impact of computers, discussed course goals and content for various segments of society. Their definition by consensus of computer literacy involved the four elements stated above plus an historical perspective of computers and future trends (2).

Figure 1.1   Personal computers of the 1980's

Photo courtesy of Radio Shack, a division of Tandy Corp., Apple Computer Corp. Inc.

In another project, the Minnesota Educational Computing Consortium (MECC) indicated the same five elements, but also felt that persons attitudes towards computers should be considered (3). Thomas Sobol and Robert Taylor in describing the Scarsdale, New York project to integrate computers into the K-12 curriculum, spoke of computers as tools to transform the schools from kindergarten upward. They advocate that pupils should begin learning about computers and computing from the time they enter school and should continue such learning through the grades (4).

We are now on the brink of a computer impact in the field of education so great that many believe it will have an impact of equal or greater magnitude upon man's intellectual development as that of reading and writing. The introduction of computing power into the educational process has the potential of providing man with universal access and rapid synthesis of knowledge as well as providing a powerful creative tool for widening man's intellectual horizon. Educators must capture the moment and decide which direction this new capability will take, rather than allowing that responsibility to be usurped by the developers of computers and computer systems. The impact of computers on education may prove to be one of the most important ethical issues man will have to deal with in the future.

EDUCATIONAL OBJECTIVES FOR COMPUTER LITERACY

Listed below are the educational objectives which will be accomplished by each chapter.

Chapter 1: What Is Computer Literacy?
The student will be able to define computer literacy.

Chapter 2: What Do People Think About Computers?
The student will be able to:

1. Describe his/her own conception about computers, including what it does as well as what it looks like.
2. Read and report on computers as represented in fiction.
3. Discuss personal attitudes towards computers.

Chapter 3: Where Did Computers Come From?
The student will be able to:

1. Realize the recent growth of computer development.
2. Identify the accomplishments of several men and women in the field.
3. Enumerate the major watersheds of computing history.
4. Make a simple counting device.

Chapter 4: How Do Computers Work?
The student will be able to:

1. Name the five major parts of a computer.
2. Explain the function of each of the five parts of the computer.
3. Discern whether or not a problem is sufficiently well defined to be solvable.
4. Define a problem sufficiently for problem solving techniques.
5. Apply the problem solving technique to a problem of daily activity.
6. Apply the problem solving technique to a math or science problem.
7. Explain how a problem is presented to the computer through a special language called a programming language.
8. Understand that there is a hierachy of computer languages.
9. Describe how a computer executes a program.
10. Write a simple program in TPL (Typical Programming Language).

Chapter 5: What Do Computers Do for Us?
The student will be able to:

1. List numerous areas of uses of computers.
2. Name one or more specific applications in each area.
3. Identify a real time application.
4. Describe one application completely including the purpose for using the computer, the environment in which it is used, the cost, the impact.
5. Make at least one visit to see a computer application in action.
6. Define *"Garbage In, Garbage Out"* and its ramifications.

Chapter 6: Where Do We Fit into the Computer Picture?
The student will be able to :

1. Identify jobs in the computer industry.
2. List the skill level required for these jobs.
3. List the educational and training requirements for these jobs.
4. Specify the environment in which these jobs take place.
5. Describe how a particular computer job has changed with changing technology.
6. Discuss their suitability to a job in the computer field.

Chapter 7: How Will Computers Affect Our Lives?
The student will be able to:

1. Define the terms privacy, automation, data bank, and computer crime.
2. Experience being identified by number.

3. Participate in instant democracy.
4. Discuss the pro's and con's of checkless/cashless society.
5. Be aware of the depersonalization and isolation which can come from interacting only with computers.
6. Define and discuss what is meant by artificial intelligence.
7. List areas in which computers will play a major role in the future.
8. Define and list uses for a personal computer.

KEY IDEAS

Computer Literacy
Microcomputers

ACTIVITIES

Take the Test
On a scale from one to ten, where one is the least and ten is the most, rate yourself on each of the computer literacy goals.

a. How computers work	1 2 3 4 5 6 7 8 9 10
b. Step-by-step techniques for problem solving	1 2 3 4 5 6 7 8 9 10
c. Social implications of computers	1 2 3 4 5 6 7 8 9 10
d. Computer applications	1 2 3 4 5 6 7 8 9 10
e. History of computing	1 2 3 4 5 6 7 8 9 10

Compute your average computer literacy. Don't worry if it is low, you can read this book to improve your score.

TEACHER'S CORNER
Purpose: To help students identify strengths and weaknesses in their knolwedge about computers.
Materials: Pencil, paper, teacher created worksheet with the computer literacy self test.
Time: 10 to 15 minutes.
Additional Information: This measure is only a self test. A graph of the results could be prepared. The test could be administered again at the end of computer studies to allow the students to note their own progress.

Twenty Questions

Listed below are twenty statements which you may or may not agree with. Indicate the extent to which you agree by circling a number from 1 to 7.

	Agree Disagree
1. Computers are always right	1 2 3 4 5 6 7
2. Computers do not have personality	1 2 3 4 5 6 7
3. Computers are more than a tool	1 2 3 4 5 6 7
4. Computers will someday be smarter than people	1 2 3 4 5 6 7
5. Computers are beginning to take over the world	1 2 3 4 5 6 7
6. Computers are making life more complex	1 2 3 4 5 6 7
7. Computers are necessary in order to solve the problems of mankind	1 2 3 4 5 6 7
8. Computers will never be able to have feelings or emotions	1 2 3 4 5 6 7
9. Someday everybody will own a computer	1 2 3 4 5 6 7
10. I would like to own a computer	1 2 3 4 5 6 7
11. I would not like talking to a computer	1 2 3 4 5 6 7
12. Computers frighten me	1 2 3 4 5 6 7
13. Computers should be developed that understand our language	1 2 3 4 5 6 7
14. Computers should not put people out of work	1 2 3 4 5 6 7
15. Only experts can use computers	1 2 3 4 5 6 7
16. Computers are fun to play with	1 2 3 4 5 6 7
17. Most people do not need to learn about computers in school	1 2 3 4 5 6 7
18. Computers think much like humans do	1 2 3 4 5 6 7
19. Computers are basically good	1 2 3 4 5 6 7
20. Computers always do as they are told	1 2 3 4 5 6 7

TEACHER'S CORNER

Purpose: To provide a means for testing attitudes about computers.

Materials: A teacher created worksheet of the questions.

Time: 20 minutes.

Skills: Reading, comprehension, self judgment.

Additional Information: This questionnaire can provide a springboard for discussion about attitudes toward computers. It is also interesting to use the questionnaire again after the computer literacy material has been covered to compare how attitudes have or have not changed.

GENERAL TEACHING RESOURCES
Books About Computers
1. Ahl, David. *Getting Started in Classroom Computing.* Digital Publishing Company.
2. Billings, Karen and Moursund, David. *Are You Computer Literate?* Dilithium Press, 1979.
3. Bork, Alfred. *Learning with Computers.* Digital Press, 1981.
4. Doerr, Christine. *Microcomputers and the 3r's.* Hayden Book Company, Inc. 1979.
5. Dunlap, Mike; Unger, Rose; Etting, Mary; Moursund, David. *Computers in Education: Resource Handbook.* University of Oregon.
6. Horn, Carin and Poirot, James. *Computer Literacy, Problem Solving with Computers.* Sterling Swift Publishing Co., 1981.
7. Hunter, Beverly; Kastner, Carol; Rubin, Martin. *Learning Alternative in U.S. Education: Where Student and Computer Meet.* Educational Technology Publications, 1975.
8. Larsen, Sally Greenwood. *Computers For Kids.* Creative Computing Press, 1980.
9. Lawson, Harold. *Understanding Computer Systems.*   Computer Science Press, 1982.
10. Taylor, Robert. *The Computer in the School: Tutor, Tool, Tutee.* Teachers College Press, 1980.
11. *TOPICS, Computer Education for Elementary and Secondary Schools.* Association for Computing Machinery, 1980.

Suggested Monthly Publications
1. *The Computing Teacher.* Computing Center, Eastern Oregon State College, LaGrande, Oregon.
2. *Creative Computing.* P.O.Box 789-M, Morristown, New Jersey.
3. *Computers in Education.* Pergamon Press, Elmsford, New York.
4. *Arithmetic Teacher.* National Council of Teachers of Mathematics (NCTM)
5. *Mathematics Teacher.* National Council of Teachers of Mathematics (NCTM)
6. *Classroom Computer News.* P.O.Box 266, Cambridge, Massachusetts.
7. *Hands On!* Technical Education Research Center, Cambridge, Massachusetts.
8. *onComputing* McGraw-Hill Publication, New York, New York.
9. *Electronic Learning.* Scholastic Magazine, New York, New York.
10. *Educational Computer Magazine.* P.O. Box 535, Cupertino, California.
11. *Electronic Education.* Electronic Communications, Tallahassee, Florida.
12. *Microcomputer Index.* Santa Clara, California.

Movies and Slides
1. *The Computer and You.* Educational Activities, Freeport, New York.

2. *Adventures of the Mind.* Children's Television International, Springfield, Virginia.
3. *Computers: From Pebbles to Programs.* Guidance Associates, New York, New York.
4. *Living with Computers.* Eye Gate Media Inc., Jamaica, New York.
5. *A Computer Glossary or Coming to Terms with the Data Processor.* Britannica Films.
6. *The Information Machine.* Modern Talking Pictures, New Hyde Park, New York.
7. *What is a Computer.* Argo Record Company, New York, New York.
8. *A Computer Glossary.* Modern Talking Pictures, New Hyde Park, New York.
9. *Art from Computers.* Control Data Corporation, Rockville Maryland.
10. *Computers.* AIMS.
11. *2001 (World of Tomorrow).* Rarigs, Inc.
12. *Some Call It Software.* Modern Talking Pictures, New Hyde Park, New York.
13. *Man and Computer, A Perspective.* Modern Talking Pictures, New Hyde Park, New York.
14. *At The Forefront.* Sperry UNIVAC Free Film Library, Blue Bell, Pennsylvania.
15. *The Catalyst.* Sperry UNIVAC Free Film Library, Blue Bell, Pennsylvania.
16. *Incredible Machine (Computer Literacy Introduction).* Bell Laboratories, New Jersey.
17. *Introduction to Digital Computers.* Sperry UNIVAC Free Film Library, Blue Bell, Pennsylvania.
18. *This Business of Numbers.* Sperry UNIVAC Free Film Library Blue Bell Pennsylvania.
19. *Don't Bother Me, I'm Learning.* McGraw Hill Films, Del Mar, California.

REFERENCES

1. Hunter, Beverly. *Computer Literacy in Grades K-8.* Human Resources Research Organization (HumRRO), presented at ADCIS, Atlanta, Georgia, March 1981.
2. Austing, Richard H. and Engle, Gerald L. *Computers and Society: Report of a Workshop.* Proceedings of COMPSAC 78, Chicago, Illinois, 1978.
3. Johnson, David; Anderson, Ronald; Hanson, Thomas; Klassen, David. *Computer Literacy—What Is It?* Minnesota Educational Consortium, St. Paul, Minnesota, 1978.
4. Sobol, Thomas and Taylor, Robert. *The Scarsdale Project: Integrating Computing into K-12 Curriculum.* Proceedings of National Educational Computing Conference (NECC/2), Norfolk, Virginia, 1980.

Chapter 2

What Do People Think about Computers?

COMPUTERS IN FICTION

The purpose of this chapter is to identify and examine the sources of information that have contributed to our knowledge and prejudices about computers. The chapter will establish what the student knows about computers and whether this knowledge is founded in fact or fiction.

We read about computers in newspapers, popular magazines, and science fiction. We see filmmakers' interpretations of computers. We laugh at the satirical descriptions. All of these sources color our opinions about computers: what they can do, what they cannot do, what they look like. There are many unresolved issues associated with the computer, and fictional treatment of the computer is often used as a vehicle for emphasizing social issues. In science fiction, for example, technical problems are often less important than the human issues. Computer science fiction frequently portrays machines that are exaggerations or projections of what they might become (Fig. 2.1).

When a computer is endowed with some human aspects, disturbing scenarios become possible. Reading about such imagined possibilities can be a bit unsettling, creating anxiety over a diminished role for human beings in an increasingly technological world. Intelligent machines often are portrayed as turning against their creators. Usually when this happens, the computer is overcome by brute force. When the computer has its own power supply, the outcome is more uncertain.

Possibly the most famous movie of recent history featuring a computer is based on the book *2001: A Space Odyssey* by Arthur Clark. In this movie, the computer is named HAL, a name coded to disguise a subtle joke. (To crack the code, merely replace the letters in the name with the letters that follow them alphabetically. So H should be replaced by I, A by B. Finally replacing the L with an M, we realize what the writer is trying to tell us.) The story line is familiar. HAL begins as a competent, friendly computer with a huge memory. HAL

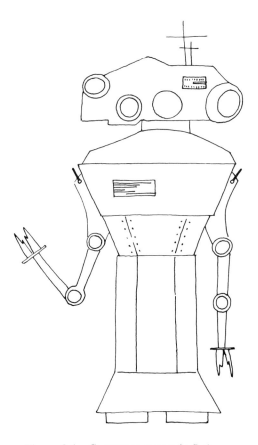

Figure 2.1   Computers as seen in fiction.

is an amusing, likable computer which gradually becomes a fierce enemy and manages to conquer his human masters in the end.

Some students will have read science fiction on their own level. Three very popular stories are *Danny Dunn and the Homework Machine* by Jay Williams, *Hold That Computer* by D. Hayes, and *The Mark of Conte* by Sonia Levitin.

In *Danny Dunn and the Homework Machine,* a professor builds a semi-portable computer called Miniac. At once, Danny calls the computer Maniac. Danny is left in charge of the computer and decides to use it for his homework. His teacher and his parents are not ready for such progress, and the story continues to an entertaining resolution.

Hold That Computer is an amusing story which combines a computer and a sports situation. Two rival schools have always been equal; neither school has been the clear winner in any sporting event. A student, Neutral Ned, suggests that the school's computer decide the impasse.

Clearly, in these two stories the computer is seen as a tool. The story line in *Hold That Computer* insists that all the data be fed to the computer, acknowledging the necessity of human intervention. In *Danny Dunn and His Homework Machine*, the computer malfunctions, causing the reader to consider the difference between computer malfunction and computer misuse.

Chaos is often the theme in computer science fiction. This can be compared with the old story of the *Sorcerer's Apprentice*, in which the aide tries to use the master's magic to make his job easier. The situation gets out of hand, with broom servants multiplying, carrying more water than needed. Fortunately, our young friend is saved by the return of the master.

In the third book, *The Mark of Conte*, chaos reigns when a student's name is recorded in the school's computer memory as Conte Mark and Mark Conte. The story depicts, in an amusing manner, the chaotic effects of this computer mix-up (Fig. 2.2).

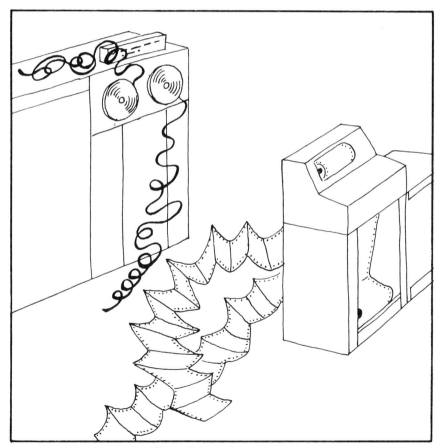

Figure 2.2 Computer chaos.

There are numerous examples of computer science fiction at the elementary and junior high school reading levels. The purpose of reviewing these books and stories is to encourage the student to think about the role that the computer plays in the story line. Was the computer beneficial to man or not? Was man in control of the computer? Do the students feel that the story line could actually happen in their lifetime?

KEY IDEAS

Science Fiction
Attitudes about Computers

ACTIVITIES

Cover Up
Make a scrapbook to hold all the materials you collect about computers. Use your imagination in designing the cover of the scrapbook.

TEACHER'S CORNER
Purpose: This project is to be assigned first, so that students will have a place for their computer-related materials.
Materials: Folders, loose-leaf notebooks, construction paper, fasteners, crayons, magic markers, tape and paste.
Time: 20-30 minutes of class time or a homework assignment.
Skills: Language, art.

Do It Yourself Computer
Use your own ideas to build a model of a computer. You may use many different materials such as boxes, wires, silver foils, bottle caps, knobs, batteries, or whatever strikes your fancy.

TEACHER'S CORNER
Purpose: This is a pre-computer literacy project. It is designed to get the student to think about their own concepts of computers.
Materials: Paper and pencils for the sketch, boxes of all shapes, scissors, glue, tape, stapler, wires, silver foil, bottle caps, knobs, batteries, tubes and cardboard rollers. The students can be encouraged to bring some of these items from home.
Time: 45 minutes of class time. This project can be one or more class periods. Projects could be completed at home.
Skills: Planning, following a plan, creative expression, teamwork.
Additional Information: Children can be encouraged to work in teams. These models can be related to a consumer awareness project by having student teams

design advertising copy which describes their features and capabilities. Students can hold mock sales, keeping records of the most popular designs.

Follow-Up: Discussion: Each student should be given an opportunity to talk about his or her model and to describe what the details on the model represent. The teacher might note how many students already have a primitive concept and vocabulary related to computers. A related activity is "Write Away."

Write Away

1. Write a short story or poem which describes how you feel about computers.

2. Write a paragraph describing a computer or robot from a movie or television show. Try to tell whether the computer or robot is helpful or harmful to people.

TEACHER'S CORNER

Purpose: This is a pre-computer literacy project. It is designed to encourage the student to think about computers as they are represented in fiction, as well as to formulate independent concepts about computers.

Materials: Paper, pencil.

Time: 20-30 minutes classtime or homework.

Skills: Writing, creative expression.

Additional Information: This activity is a good follow-up to the "Do It Yourself Computer" activity. It helps the child to focus on the issue of computers as a positive or negative tool for people and society.

Watchdog

Start collecting articles, stories and pictures about computers from newspapers and magazines.

TEACHER'S CORNER

Purpose: This is a computer awareness project which encourages the child to look for the computers in current events.

Materials: Magazines, newspapers, brochures, paper, paste, scissors, and glue for mounting.

Time: Ongoing project.

Skills: Reading, research.

Additional Information: These articles could be used as the basis for a class bulletin board or could be stored in the student scrapbook. These articles will be a resource for activities in Chapters 5 and 7. Students might want to share current events articles on a regular basis.

For the Bookworm
WRITE A BOOK REPORT

Use your favorite book about computers. This book can be a science fiction or factual book.

DESIGN A BOOK JACKET
    Create a jacket for a book about computers. Remember that a book jacket includes information about the book and author on the inside leaves.

TEACHER'S CORNER
Purpose: This is a pre-computer literacy project which emphasizes computers in fact and fiction.
Materials: Paper, pencil, construction paper and crayons.
Time: Homework assignment; two weeks for reading time and report preparation.
Skills: Reading, writing, creative expression.

Cub Reporter
Interview five people in your school to find out their opinions about computers. Try to interview the principal, some teachers and students, the school health officer, the librarian, and other school aides. You might ask them questions such as

1. Have you ever used a computer?
2. Do you think computers will be helpful to our school?
3. Do you think computers are helpful in our daily lives?

These interviews would make interesting articles for a school newspaper.

TEACHER'S CORNER
Purpose: This computer awareness project will help the student realize that there are many different opinions about computers.
Materials: Paper, pencil.
Time: One week project.
Skills: Verbal and written communication.
Additional Information: These articles could be used together with the articles written for the activity, ''What's the Scoop?,'' in Chapter 3 in order to form a class newsletter.

Suggestion Box
Make a list of 5 things you want to learn about computers. Share your list with your classmates.

1. _____
2. _____
3. _____
4. _____
5. _____

TEACHER'S CORNER

Purpose: This pre-computer literacy project is designed to stimulate student interest in the "computer fun" to come.

Materials: A teacher created ditto of this activity for each student, pencils.

Time: 20 minutes.

Skills: Writing, thinking, sharing.

Additional Information: This activity lends itself well to a learning center with a suggestion box where students can drop their questions and ideas.

RELATED READINGS

(**S** -Student, **T** -Teacher)

1. Ahl, David. *The Colossal Computer Cartoon Book.* Creative Computing, 1977. (**S,T**)
2. Bailey, Richard. *Computer Poems.* Potagannissing Press, 1973. (**S,T**)
3. Dodson, Fitzhugh. *I Wish I Had a Computer That Makes Waffles.* Oak Tree Publications, 1978. (**S,T**)
4. Godfrey, David. *Guttenburg Two.* University of Victoria Press, 1980. (**T**)
5. Mowshowitz, Abbe. *Inside Information, Computers in Fiction.* Addison Wesley Publishing Company, 1977. (**T**)
6. Van Tassel, Dennie. *The Compleat Computer.* Science Research Associates, Inc., 1976. (**T**)
7. Van Tassel, Dennie. *Computers, Computers, Computers: In Fiction and in Verse.* Elsevier, 1977. (**T**)

Stories For Your Students

1. Bova, Ben. *Escape.* Holt, Rinehart & Winston, 1970.
2. Butterworth, William. *Next Stop, Earth.* Walker & Company, 1978.
3. Dick, Philip. *Autofac.* Thomas Nelson, 1973.
4. Hayes, Dick. *Hold That Computer.* Atheneum, 1968.
5. Higdon, Hal. *The Electronic Olympics.* Holt Rinehart & Winston, 1972.
6. Levitin, Sonia. *The Mark of Conte.* Atheneum, 1979.
7. MacGregor, Ellen. *Miss Pickerell Meets Mr. H.U.M.* McGraw-Hill, 1974.
8. Nourse, Alan E. *Star Surgeon.* David McKay Company, 1966.
9. Philbrook, Clem. *Ollie's Team and the Baseball Computer.* Hastings Howe, 1967.
10. Silverberg, Robert (editor). *Beyond Control.* Elsevier, 1973.
11. Slote, Alfred. *My Robot Buddy.* Avon Books, 1975.
12. Slote, Alfred. *My Trip to Alpha I.* J. B. Lippincott Company, 1978.
13. Sundh, Kerstin. *Augusta Can Do Anything.* Putnam, 1973.
14. Tenn, Williams. *Child's Play.* Thomas Nelson, 1970.
15. Williams, Jay, Abrashkin, Raymond. *Danny Dunn and the Homework Machine.* McGraw-Hill, 1958.

16. Williams, Jay, Abrashkin, Raymond. *Danny Dunn and the Voice From Space*. McGraw-Hill, 1959.
17. Yolen, Jane. *The Robot and Rebecca*. Alfred A. Knopf, 1980.

Chapter 3

Where Did Computers Come From?

THE HISTORY OF COMPUTATION

To appreciate the current state of the art and identify future trends, it is important to take a look backward and see where we have come from. The purpose of this chapter is to do just that: to help the student understand the background of computing and its rapid growth, identify the accomplishments of several men and women who made significant contributions to the field of computing, and enumerate the major watersheds of computing.

In the earliest days of computing, computational devices were used mainly for scientific and mathematical calculations; only later in the development of these devices was their use turned toward other applications. Computers as we know them today have been on the scene only since the late 1930's or early 1940's, when they too were used mainly for scientific and mathematical calculations. Within just a few years, we have come to use the computer in almost every discipline imaginable.

The history of computing begins with primitive people using fingers and toes as counting aids. From that beginning followed the writings and scratches on cave walls (Fig. 3.1). When it became too cumbersome to "carry around the wall of the cave" to show how many dinosaur bones had been collected or dragons had been killed, early cave dwellers started using pebbles or sticks to represent the items that they wanted to count or enumerate. For example, three pebbles might mean three clubs at home.

The Romans wanted to be able to represent the number of items traded in a financial transaction. They began to use a **tally stick,** which was a wooden stick scored down the center (Fig. 3.2). For each item a notch was made horizontally crossing the center score. The stick was separated at the center when the transaction was finished, one Roman taking one piece, the other taking the other. The Romans also conducted business and recorded numbers on wax and wood tablets.

Figure 3.1   Early cave writings showed the representation of quantities.

The Chinese had not invented the abacus at this time, as is commonly thought, but were using a suan pan, a reckoning board much like the Roman tally stick. In fact the abacus was first developed by the Egyptians and the Hindus, almost simultaneously, in the 10th Century B.C.

The Egyptians were known for using **sand grooves** to record and represent numbers. For example, they would make three grooves in the sand and then fill them with pebbles, one for each item to be represented (Fig. 3.3). When they wanted to add to this pattern, they added column by column starting at the right hand column, carrying when necessary. They truly had the rudiments of a good system, although it was hardly a portable one. When the Egyptians put their sand grooves and pebbles into a box, the first abacus was made.

The **abacus** as we know it today was not perfected by the Chinese until over 2000 years later, in the 12 Century A.D. The abacus can be called a bi-quinque device, as it relys on two (bi) groups of five (quinque). The abacus is still in use today and is very easy to use. (See "You Can Count On It" activity for a description of the construction and use of the abacus). Great races are often held today between an abacus user and a user of the most modern calculator, with the abacus user often scoring very high.

At this point in computing history developments occurred in two areas at once: one toward the creation of mechanical devices, and the other toward the

Figure 3.2 Transaction using the Roman tally stick.

formulation of number schemes more sophisticated than the scratchings and pebbles.

NUMBER SYSTEMS

In the beginning people described a quantity in such a way that the number and the article were of equal importance. For example *4 apples* was distinct because it was apples, as well as because it was 4. Such concrete numbers gradually disappeared as people became able to deal with abstract ideas and developed abstract **number systems.** Early schemes differed greatly from our number system today in shape, style and even in base. Number systems developed in different locations were different from each other because they were influenced by the culture of the society the system was developed to serve. Table 3.1 lists the people and their early system.

Two basic types of number systems developed, the **tally system** in which

Figure 3.3   Pebbles in a sand groove.

the same symbol is used over and over, and the **code system** in which different numbers have different symbols (Fig. 3.4).

PEOPLE	NUMBER BASE	COMMENTS
Chinese	2	first known base two system, then forgotten
Mesopotanians	3	one of the few known trinary number systems
Egyptian	5	based on the hand, a sacred symbol of the Middle East
American Indian	20	probably based on fingers and toes
Babylonian	60	largest known number base

Table 3.1   Early cultures and their number bases.

Eventually a third type of number system evolved which was based on **place value.**

Chinese (Code System)

The Chinese number system originally had two as its base. This has since been lost. Figure 3.5 shows examples of the Chinese symbols used today.

Roman (Tally System)

We are familar with the Roman numerals (Fig. 3.6).

NUMBER	TALLY	CODE
1	I	A
2	II	B
3	III	C

Figure 3.4 Examples of a tally system versus a code system of numbers.

1	—	20	
2	=	30	
3	≡	40	
4	八	400	
5	五	4000	

Figure 3.5 Chinese number symbols. The Chinese differentiated values by an accompanying suffix, i.e., ┼ meant 10's, 百 meant 100's, and 千 meant 1000's.

The original symbol for 4 was IIII and only later did it change to IV. The symbols were chosen because of their relation to the world at that time. The symbols I II III IIII look very much like the hand signals for those numbers. The C for 100 came, perhaps, from the Latin word Centum which means 100. The Roman numbering scheme was mainly a recording technique, not meant for nor usable in calculating, because there was no way to represent zero! That was to come later.

I	1
II	2
III	3
IIII	4
V	5
C	100

Figure 3.6 The Roman tally system.

Egyptian (Code System)
The Egyptians wrote on papyrus scrolls. The oldest known scroll with numbers is called the RHIND papyrus. It is also called the Ahmes papyrus after the scribe, Ahmes. The papyrus dates from 1600 BC. Figure 3.7 illustrates the symbols used by the early Egyptians.

1	I	1,000	
2	II	10,000	
10	∩	100,000	
100	⟋	1,000,000	

Figure 3.7 Early Egyptian symbols.

These symbols, too, have cultural meaning: the staff of wheat for numbers 1 to 9; the heel of a foot, which we can associate with the idea of ten toes, for the number 10; the coiled hemp rope, a valuable commodity, for 100; the flowers; the pointing finger; and finally the astonished man. Wouldn't you be astonished if you had 1,000,000 items?

Babylonian (Tally System)
The Babylonian number system base, 60, is the largest known to man. Odd as it may seem, even today we use the base 60 in many of our calculations. It is used

in time, as 60 minutes in an hour, and in the measurement of angles. The Babylonian system is often called the cuneiform, from the Latin CUNEUS meaning a wedge. The Babylonians used only two symbols ▼, and ▾ .

How did they show numbers greater than 59? They were the first to use the concept of place value.

To express the number 133 in the Babylonian system:

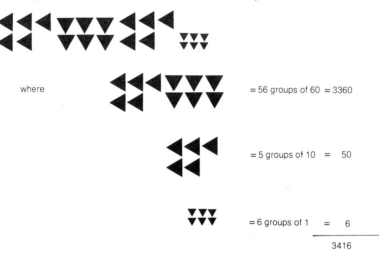

To express the number 3416 in the Babylonian system:

They did have one problem which surely has occurred to you. How could they distinguish between 3601 and 61. The problem was finally solved by using a "." to symbolize a missing symbol other than in the ones place.

To express the number 62 in the Babylonian system:

To express the number 3602 in the Babylonian system:

They almost had the concept of zero but not quite. They never used the dot in the one's place.

Mayan (Tally System)

The Mayans knew that a good numbering system needed a zero. The Mayans were living in the western hemisphere in the time well before any transatlantic travel. It is doubtful that they influenced or were influenced by any other peoples. They effectively used the symbol ".". Figure 3.8 depicts their number system.

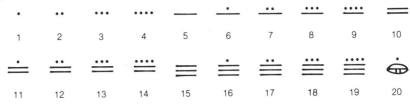

Figure 3.8   The Mayan number system.

Using the symbol ⬭, which meant 20, they moved the dot to new positions to have the effect of place value. The number of dots indicated the number of 20's for this value.

⬭ = 2 groups of 20, or 40

Greek (Code System)

The Greeks used a code system of 27 symbols from which they created 999 combinations (Fig. 3.9). A code system has no place value.

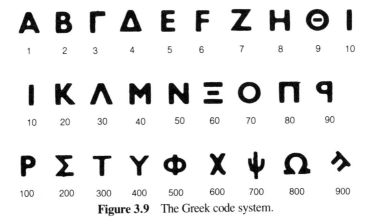

Figure 3.9   The Greek code system.

It is mainly from code number systems like the Greek and the Hebrew that superstitions about numbers (we could call them numberstitions) developed. To form a certain number, combine the symbols so that their representative sum is the desired number. When doing this you can occasionally make a word. Often mystical powers or meanings would be associated with that number. For example the Hebrew number ‎ חי is 18. The word CHAI means life so the number 18 is thought to be special to the Hebrews as a symbol of life.

Hindu (Place Value System)
The figures that we use today came from the Hindus. The Moors, who knew the Hindu and Arabic world, brought the numbering system with them to their great universities. In the last years of the 900's, Gerbert of Auxillac (who later became known as Pope Sylvester II) wanted very much to study at the great universities of the Moors at Cordova or Sevilla. No Christian was allowed to study there. Gerbert professed to no longer be associated with Christianity and was then allowed to enter. He lived among the Moors, studied and graduated from the university and then returned to the Christian world, bringing with him the Arabic number system.

The Hindu number for two is $=$. If you write it over and over and you get a bit careless, it begins to look like our number 2. Likewise the Hindu $\equiv$ is a 3. The system was a code system which incorporated both place value and the idea of a zero. The advantage of such a place value number system is that it provides an easy way of noting the magnitude of a given number. For example, the Roman numeral for 8, VIII, appears bigger than the Roman numeral for 10, X if we look only at the number of symbols needed to express the number. In the Hindu/Arabic system, which uses the place value system, the number 8 is "smaller", that is it has fewer digits, than the number 10. Table 3.2 compares the Hindu, Arabic and modern symbols.

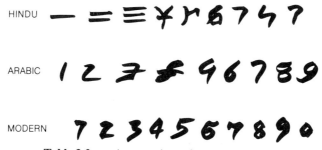

Table 3.2   A comparison of number symbols.

Binary Number System (Place Value System)
From about 1000 A.D. until the late 1800's there were no new developments in number systems. All of the mechanical calculators in use during that time period used the modern version of the Arabic number system. It was in the 1880's that an Englishwoman named Lady Lovelace created the **binary number system.** The system is based on two symbols: the zero and a one. Like our decimal system, place value is the key to the binary system.

To express the quantity 0 in the binary number system, write 0_2 . To express the quantity 1, write 1_2 . How is a value greater than 1 shown? Since there are no more symbols left to use, it becomes necessary to use one of the symbols over again in a new place where the symbol will represent greater value. Therefore to show the quantity 2, 10_2, or one group of two and no groups of one. Likewise, the quantity 3 is shown as 11_2 , or one group of two and one group of one. To show the quantity 4, we again need to use the theory of place value, so that 100_2 is one group of four, no group of two and no group of one.

10111_2 in binary means (from right to left):

$$\begin{array}{ll}
1 \text{ group of ones } = & 1 \\
1 \text{ group of twos } = & 2 \\
1 \text{ group of 4 } \quad = & 4 \\
0 \text{ group of 8 } \quad = & 0 \\
1 \text{ group of 16 } \quad = & 16 \\
\hline
& 23 \text{ in the base } 10
\end{array}$$

It was not until the advent of the truly electronic computers that a number system other than the decimal one was necessary. The binary number system was very "natural" for the electronic computer. An electric pulse ⌐‾⌐ would be symbolized by a 1 and the absence of the pulse ——— by a zero, accordingly, ⌐‾‾⌐‾⌐ would mean 1011_2 in binary.

COMPUTATIONAL DEVICES

From the first appearance of the abacus to the early 1600's, no new calculating devices were developed. To understand why advances began during the 1600's, it is important to know what was going on in the world at that time. The Dark Ages were over, the age of exploration had begun, and Columbus had discovered the New World on his way to a new route to the East. Trade with the New World had begun, and life was becoming more complicated than ever before. At the beginning of the 1600's, a Scotsman named John Napier developed logarithms. These numbers were engraved on white rods in order to allow easy manipulation, especially in multiplication and division. These rods came to be known as Napier's bones (Fig. 3.10).

Automatic Calculating Machines

In early 1620 in Tubingen, Germany, Wilhelm Schickard designed a machine that would automatically add and subtract, and perform multiplication and division in a semi-automatic manner. We know about Schickard because in 1624 he sent a letter and a copy of his design to the great scientist of the day, Johannes Kepler. Schickard's machine had gears for the accumulator as well as a place where unconnected gears could be used to enter numbers directly in a manual way. This feature, the ability to manually enter a number which would then be incorporated into the calculation, allowed for more rapid multiplication than was known before. He also included 6 cylinders on which were to be engraved the multiplication tables of Napier. Unfortunately, the machine was destroyed

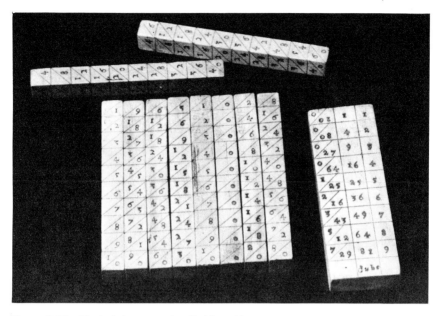

Figure 3.10 Napier's bones used to find logarithms.

Smithsonian Institution photo No. 58996-C.

in a fire before it was finished. Schickard was not a lucky man. He and his entire family died during the plague that ravaged Europe during the Thirty Years' War. Save for the letter to Kepler and some records from the machinist, little was known about this man outside of his small town in central Europe.

In the 1640's, Blaise Pascal, a Frenchman aged 16, went to work for his father who was an import-export tariff collecter. Pascal saw a need to ease his father's workload. Necessity being the true mother of invention, he invented an adding wheel based on gear ratios (Fig. 3.11). The wheel was able to do subtraction as well. His wheel is the ancestor of the odometer in the cars of today. There is no reason to believe that Pascal knew anything of the work of Schickard.

Later in the century, in Germany, Gottfried Wilhelm von Leibnitz, a great scientist and mathematician, wanted to lighten the burden of astronomers and other scientists. His mechanical device allowed the user to automatically multiply and divide, enabling the laborious calculations of logarithms to be done at a rapid pace (Fig. 3.12). His machine formed the foundation for the first successful **calculator.**

The major advance made by Leibnitz was that a multiplication digit could be entered beforehand. With a turn of a crank, that number could be added to the number already in the accumulator. This design reduced multiplication to a series of handle turns.

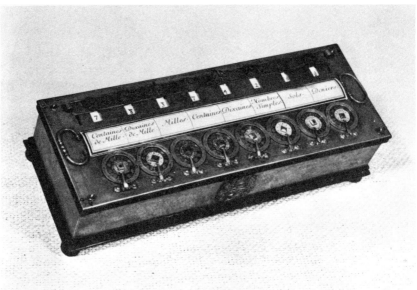

Figure 3.11   Blaise Pascal and his calculator which could perform addition and subtraction by turning a set of wheels.   *Courtesy of IBM Corp.*

The work of these three men (Schickard, Pascal, and Leibnitz) form the **first watershed** in the history of computing. They proved by the development of their machines that **arithmetic could be automated.**

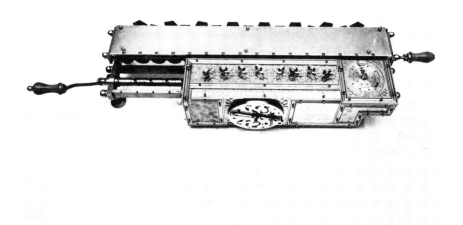

Figure 3.12 Gottfried Wilhelm von Leibnitz and his calculator which could perform multiplication and division directly.   *Courtesy of IBM Corp.*

Program Controlled Devices

It almost appears as if the world needed time to absorb these great advances, because nothing happened again until the early 1800's. At that time in France, the home of the great weaving and textile industry, skilled workers for the looms were not readily available. Already in existence was the idea of creating a mechanism to control a sequence so that a job could be reduced to a series of steps done in a routine order. This is seen in the great clocks of Europe or in the music boxes of the period (Fig. 3.13).

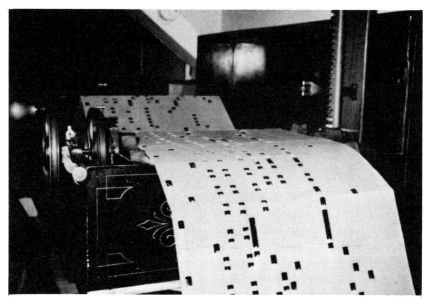

Figure 3.13   An example of one of the earliest music boxes from the Musee Baud S.A. in L'Auberson, Switzerland.   *Photo by S. Heller.*

These cylinders were seen as integral parts of the machine they were controlling. Joseph Marie Jacquard used this idea to develop a system of **punched cards** to control the pattern of the weaving. Until this time two people were needed to operate the loom, one to swing the shuttle and one to lift the threads. Jacquard's system, an extension of a system developed by silk master Basile Bouchon, operated the lifting of the threads and thus reduced the number of operators to one per machine (Fig. 3.14). By 1814, 11,000 machines were available in France, many having been converted from the worker-driven models. Soon many skilled workers found themselves without work. As automated weaving spread to England, groups of people called Luddites, who opposed the spreading **automation,** roamed the countryside destroying the machines as they come upon them. In the short span of ten years from 1804 to 1814, Jacquard was transformed from a highly acclaimed hero, awarded a medal by the king, to a villain of automation.

At about the same time in England, Charles Babbage was working on several revolutionary ideas. He is called the father of modern electronic digital computing. In 1832 he invented a Difference Engine to generate logarithmic and astronomical tables to 6 places (Fig. 3.15). Babbage, the son of a London banker, used a set of linked adding machines that were capable of automatically

Figure 3.14   The Jacquard loom, controlled by punched cards and operated by only one worker, can produce complicated patterns in fabric. This loom is in use in China.

Photo by Barbara Friedman.

calculating successive values of algebraic functions. The technique he used was the computation of successive differences, hence the name Difference Engine. By 1822 Babbage had a small working version of the engine that could handle functions of the second order. In fact, that engine was the only one ever completed successfully. Joseph Clement, a toolmaker, was hired to build the complete Difference Engine, but the design was beyond even his master skills of the day. It should be noted that, though the machinist was unable to build the necessary parts, the intricate design of the Difference Engine served to advance the level of machinery skills of the time.

Based on Babbage's fine work and his fine reputation (he was awarded the first gold medal ever offered by the Royal Astronomical Society), he was able to get financial backing to carry out further work on an Analytical Engine to be powered by steam (Fig. 3.16). This engine was to operate on punched cards like the Jacquard loom. Babbage envisioned a data storage section, an arithmetic calculating section, a data input section and a printing section. Unfortunately his work was never completed. However, its merit was recognized after Babbage's death in an 1879 report from the Merryfield Committee appointed to consider the advisability and estimate the expense of constructing the Analytical Engine. This report noted that ''...apart from the question of its saving labour in operations now possible,...existence of such an instrument would place within

Figure 3.15   Charles Babbage and his Difference Engine which was used to produce mathematical tables.   *Courtesy of IBM Corp.*

reach much which if not actually impossible, has been too close to the limits of human skill and endurance to be practically available.''

The **second watershed** of computing history is marked by Babbage's concept that a **computing device could be programmed:** that is, it could be built in such a manner as to accomplish a long series of arithmetic and decision

Figure 3.16 A model of the Analytical Engine, designed by Babbage, which would have accepted information from punched cards, stored the program inside and printed the results automatically. *Courtesy of IBM Corp.*

operations without human intervention. The other machines of Babbage's day could do only one calculation at a time.

Charles Babbage was a great friend of Lady Ada Lovelace, an accomplished mathematician and the only child of Lord Byron. She encouraged Babbage in his work and has been called the first programmer. In 1842 she began to translate into French Babbage's notes on the Analytical Engine. She added her own ideas as she worked, ending with a document three times longer than the original (Fig. 3.17). She spent most of her energy trying to advance people's understanding of Babbage's work. She tried often to restate his ideas simply enough for the working man to grasp. During this time she developed the system of binary numbers. Lady Lovelace's accomplishments in mathematics were highly unusual for a woman in the 19th century. It is interesting to note that her father, Lord Byron, a patron of the Luddites, was as much an adversary of automation as she was a champion of the cause.

Tabulating Machines and the 1890 Census

In the year 1880, in full compliance with the dictates of the Constitution, the United States began the once-a-decade census. It took nine years to tabulate this census. In the meantime the leaders in Washington became very concerned: The country was growing rapidly and there was concern about the task of completing the 1890 census. In 1884 Herman Hollerith, at age 19, was appointed to as-

Figure 3.17   Lady Ada Lovelace, the first programmer.

sist Professor William Trowbridge of Columbia University in solving this problem (Fig. 3.18).

Hollerith developed a simple **tabulating machine** that worked as follows. At the front of the machine was a large replica of a punched card with the meaning of all the squares delineated, item by item. To record information, the operator moved the punching mechanism to the correct spot. When all the information was entered on the card, the card was placed in a card reader which had small finger-like pins that came down from above. Wherever there was a hole on the card, the pins came in contact with a pool of mercury below thus closing an electric circuit. This caused a count to advance. Then a correct slot opened so that the information could be automatically sorted by vital statistic.

The first patent was issued in 1884 for this **tabulator**, which integrated many of the ideas of earlier devices, especially the Jacquard loom and the punched cards used by the railroads. Prior to 1890 Hollerith's machine was tested on mortality data in Baltimore and New York; then it was used to recalculate the 1880 census in competition with two nonmechanical systems in vogue at the time. Hollerith's system won hands down. His tabulator was used successfully in the 1890 census (Fig. 3.19). It took only two and one half years to finish the census using 56 million cards. (The country's leadership was not very happy with the results because the census showed that the population had not grown as much as expected.) In 1896 Hollerith returned to his native Albany and founded the Tabulating Machine Company which he sold in 1911. In 1924

Figure 3.18 Herman Hollerith, inventor of automatic tabulating machines.

this company merged to form the International Business Machines (IBM) Corporation. Hollerith's device was used in census tabulation around the world by the end of 1800's. A sad footnote to this is that 90 percent of the historic 1890 census was destroyed in a major warehouse fire.

Advent of the Modern Computer
The next events in computing history occurred as a result of the two World Wars. In the early 1930's Konrad Zuse, a German, worked as a pioneer in the area of general-purpose, program controlled computers, but all of his work remained unknown until after World War II. Because of this it is often noted that the next breakthrough was at Harvard University. In the mid 1930's Howard Aiken, then a graduate student in the Department of Physics, designed an automatic computing machine to help solve differential equations necessary for his thesis. Working with him on the MARK I was Grace Hopper (Fig. 3.20). Together they arranged for the building of the machine by IBM. The MARK I was hailed as Babbage's dream come true. Unfortunately it did not include any decision making ability, even though, in the Analytical Engine, Babbage had suggested such an idea.

The MARK I was an electromechanical device, that is, a device whose moving mechanical parts are driven by electricity. It was very big, 50 feet long with 500 miles of wire (Fig. 3.21). The MARK I was in operation until 1959 at Harvard. Grace Hopper recently recounted an incident that took place when the MARK I failed to operate. Finding the problem proved to be a difficult pro-

Figure 3.19   Automation of the 1890 census using Hollerith devices.

Courtesy of the Library of Congress.

cedure. Finally, after many hours, a small insect was found creeping around in one of the relays of the MARK I. The researchers extricated it, taped it in the log book of the experiment, and dubbed the incident the first computer **debugging.**

Figure 3.20   Grace Hopper, an early pioneer of computer technology.

Courtesy of the U.S. Navy.

Figure 3.21   A model of the MARK I, the first modern computer, built by IBM at Harvard University. It was an automatic sequence controlled calculator operated by a series of relays.   *Smithsonian Institution photo No. 62971.*

World tensions prior to World War II produced the need for faster and faster calculations. Until 1972 it was thought that the first truly electronic digital computer was the ENIAC developed between 1939 and 1944 by J. Presper Eckert, Jr. and John W. Mauchly. However, a patent lawsuit in 1972 determined that "Eckert and Mauchly did not themselves first invent the automatic electronic digital computer, but instead derived that subject matter from one Dr. John Vincent Atanasoff."   The Atanasoff Berry Computer, the ABC, was developed between 1935 and 1942 while Atanasoff and his graduate student, Clifford Berry, were at Iowa State University (Fig. 3.22).

Figure 3.22   Dr. John Atanasoff and the Atanasoff Berry Computer (ABC) which was the forerunner of electronic computer technology.   *Courtesy of Iowa State University.*

The successor, ENIAC, was a secret wartime computer which had no mechanical parts, no counters, no wheels (Fig. 3.23). It used on-off electric circuits, took up two floors of the Moore School of Electrical Engineering of the University of Pennsylvania and worked, very slowly by today's standards. ENIAC had 70,000 resistors, 10,000 capacitors, 18,000 thermionic valves. If a valve failed, it took as much as 8 hours just to find which one it was. All of that electric power turned quickly into heat, so that the ENIAC could not be run for more that one hour at a time. Even so ENIAC could do in one hour what MARK I could do in one week. It has been said that when the power was turned on for the ENIAC, the lights in Philadelphia dimmed.

Figure 3.23   Dr. J. Presper Eckert, Jr. examines the automatic control panel of ENIAC.
Courtesy of the Library of Congress.

Until the mid 1940's, each command to be executed by the computer had to be entered into the computer as a tedious sequence of switches. The **third watershed** in computing history occurred in 1946 when Dr. John von Neumann (Fig. 3.24) suggested that a **set of instructions or commands could be stored within the computer** just as the data could be stored and that the computer could even modify the instructions automatically. The first computer to incorporate the concept of a **stored program** was developed at the University of Manchester. The EDSAC (Electronic Delay Storage Automatic Computer) was smaller that the ENIAC but 6 times faster. The commands were not done by setting switches, but rather, were read in from a paper tape punched with the proper code.

Generations of Computers
From then on the development of computing devices occurred very rapidly, moving from one computer generation to next. The first generation of electronic computers, from 1946 to 1952, was characterized by the large **vacuum tube** computer. By today's standards they were slow and cumbersome. They generated a great deal of heat and therefore were always housed in air-conditioned rooms. The second generation, from 1952 to the early 1960's, was marked by the introduction of **transistors.** The transistor, developed by the

Figure 3.24   Dr. John von Neumann, who formally stated the concept of the stored program computer.

Bell Telephone Laboratories, was used instead of vacuum tubes. It allowed more rapid calculation, larger memory, and more powerful computing capabilities, while being physically smaller (Fig. 3.25).

The third generation of computers began in the late 1960's with the use of **integrated circuits** (IC). With ICs, entire electric circuits are imprinted and held on a small card or **chip.** The fourth generation, marked by the ultra **miniaturization** of the 1970's, ushered in the very large memory computer with reasonable physical size. For example, Honeywell Corporation recently announced that it could put the equivalent of 200,000 transistors on a slice of silicon the size of a thumbtack.

This miniaturization led to a large enough memory to realize the **multiprogramming** concept, the ability for more than one program to operate on the computer at once (Fig. 3.26 and Table 3.3).

Many computer scientists feel we are now in the fifth generation, a rapidly evolving era of computer specialization and the home **microcomputer** explosion (Fig. 3.27).

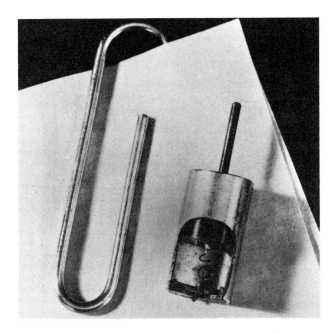

Figure 3.25 Comparison of the size of a transistor and a paper clip.

Courtesy of the Library of Congress.

Year	Technology	Components per cu. ft.	Computer additions per sec.
1947	Large vacuum tubes	320	3,500
1953	Smaller vacuum tubes	2,000	17,000
1960	Transistors	15,000	229,000
1964	Miniaturized transistor logic	30,000	2,500,000

Table 3.3 A comparison of size and speed of computer components.

Figure 3.26 The CRAY computer, the world's largest computer capable of over 80,000,000 operations per second.   *Courtesy of CRAY Research, Inc.*

Figure 3.27   The Piccolo, a modern microcomputer manufactured in Denmark.
Courtesy of Regnecentralen Computer Corp.

Key Ideas

Computer
Tally Stick
Sand Groove
Abacus

Number Systems:
  Tally System
  Code System
  Place Value
  Binary System
Calculator
Punched Cards
Tabulator
Automation
Three Watersheds:
  Automated Arithmetic
  Automated Instructions
  Stored Program Computer
Debug
Vacuum Tube
Transistor
Integrated Circuit
Chip
Multiprogramming
Microcomputer

ACTIVITIES

History Highlights
HALL OF FAME
   Prepare a bulletin board computer "Hall of Fame" with pictures (or draw-ings) and paragraphs about famous people and events in computing history.

TEACHER'S CORNER
Purpose: This activity focuses attention on important people and events in the history of computing.
Materials: Construction paper, magic markers, crayons, staples, tape, glue.
Time: Ongoing project.
Skills: Writing, sequencing, research, reading, creative expression, organization.

Additional Information: This activity could be integrated with the "World View" and "Timely Line" activities by setting aside a display area, created by the students, to include all three activities.

WORLD VIEW
Take a map of the world and locate the places where important events in computing history took place.

TEACHER'S CORNER
Purpose: This activity focuses on a geographical study of the history of computing.
Materials: World map, markers or pins.
Time: Ongoing project.
Skills: Map skills, research.
Additional Information: See "Hall of Fame."

TIMELY LINE
Make a history time line. Include important events in computing history and world history (from social studies). If you are making your own history time line, be sure to include important dates in your family such as birthdays and weddings.

TEACHER'S CORNER
Purpose: This activity focuses on the chronology of the history of computing.
Materials: Construction paper, used computer paper, markers, crayons.
Time: Ongoing project.
Skills: Reading, research, chronology.
Additional Information: See "Hall of Fame."

WHAT'S THE SCOOP?
Pretend you are a newspaper reporter covering an important event in computing history. Write a newspaper article about this event, telling the important facts: Who? What? Where? When? and How?

TEACHER'S CORNER
Purpose: This activity provides the opportunity for a student to research one event or individual in detail.
Time: One week homework assignment.
Skills: Research, reading, writing.

ACTING UP
Work with a partner to prepare a skit telling about a major event in computing history.

TEACHER'S CORNER
Purpose: This activity provides the opportunity for a student to research one event or individual in detail.
Time: One week homework assignment.
Skills: Research, creative writing, speech, dramatics.

SCRAMBLED EGGS
Make a list of any 10 events or people you can remember from computing history. Scramble your list and give it to a classmate to unscramble into the correct order.

TEACHER'S CORNER
Purpose: Review of the history of computing.
Materials: Teacher created worksheet.
Time: 30 minutes.
Skills: Chronology, memory, recall.

Numerous Numbers
DOWN THE NILE
Using a chart of Egyptian number symbols, convert Egyptian number symbols into decimal numbers and convert decimal numbers into Egyptian number symbols. Express the Egyptian numbers below as decimal numbers.

Express these decimal numbers in Egyptian code system.
a. 1,000,001   b. 843   c. 20,117

TEACHER'S CORNER
Purpose: To illustrate how quantities can be represented by different number systems.
Materials: Teacher created worksheet.
Time: 30-40 minutes.
Skills: Abstract reasoning, quantification.
Additional Information: A third level of conversion could be made to produce a class chart of Egyptian, decimal, and binary number equivalents. This chart could be expanded to include as many number systems as desired.

TRIBAL NUMBERS
Find out about a Native American tribe that lived in your area. Learn how they counted and how they wrote numbers.

TEACHER'S CORNER
Purpose: This activity relates number systems information to local history.

Time: Homework project.
Skill: Research.
Additional Information: Contact the Public Information Staff, Bureau of Indian Affairs, 18th and C Streets NW, Washington, D.C. 20240 for the name of local Indian tribes.

CRACK THE CODE

Make a code number system using:

A	B	C	D	E	F	G	H	I	J	K	L	M	N	O	P	Q
1	2	3	4	5	6	7	8	9	10	20	30	40	50	60	70	80

R	S	T	U	V	W	X	Y	Z
90	100	200	300	400	500	600	700	800

Invent some numberstitions (lucky and unlucky numbers) of your own using this code number system.

TEACHER'S CORNER
Purpose: To illustrate how quantities can be represented by different symbols.
Time: 30 minutes of class time or homework assignment.
Skill: Abstract reasoning.

BE A MATH BEE
Using the Mayan number system, have a Math Bee to see which team can convert the most numbers from Mayan number system to the decimal number system in five minutes. Use these numbers to get started:

a. b. c.

TEACHER'S CORNER
Purpose: To give the students a chance to try their skill at number system conversion.
Materials: Poster with the numbers in the Mayan system, stopwatch.
Time: 15 minutes (for a mini bee, reduce the time).
Skills: Grouping, addition, abstraction.
Additional Information: The teacher can run a Math Bee using any number system. A truly challenging bee would ask teams to convert from a place value system such as the binary system to a code or tally number system. To make this conversion, students may find it helpful to first convert to the decimal system.

Stand Up And Be Counted
With three of your classmates, show how a binary counter would work by counting from 0 to 8.

TEACHER'S CORNER
Description: Four students stand in a line, each with a placard. The placard has a zero on one side and a one on the other. Each student represents a power of two place value in the binary number system. Initially all the placards facing the class are at zero. When the teacher claps once, the first place person (at the extreme right facing the class) flips the placard to the one side. On the next clap the first place person flips the card to the zero side and nudges the person to his right who flips his card. Every time a child turns the card so that a one is facing him, he will nudge the person next to him as a signal to flip the card. On every clap, the first place person flips his card.
Purpose: Drill and practice in binary counting.
Materials: Four posters, each with a one on one side and a zero on the other.
Time: 15 minutes.
Skills: Following directions, place value concepts.
Additional Information: This is a good lead-in activity to many of the binary number activities.

Binary Magic
Make a set of four cards as shown:

C	O	D	E
8 9 10 11	4 5 6 7	2 3 6 7	1 3 5 7
12 13 14 15	12 13 14	10 11 14	9 11 13
	15	15	15

Ask a friend to think of a number from 1 to 15. Show your friend the cards in such a way that you cannot see them. Ask if the number is on the "C" card, the "O" card, the "D" card, or the "E" card. Once you have been told which card(s) the number is on, you will know the number. (The trick is in the binary number system. If the number is on the "C" card, the number has one group of 8's in it; on the "O" card one group of 4's; on the "D" card one group of 2's; and finally on the "E" card one group of 1's. If your friend had picked the number 10, it would be on the "C" card and on the "D" card. You would add one group of 8's and one group of 2's, or 8+2, for 10, and you've performed MAGIC!)

TEACHER'S CORNER
Purpose: Drill and practice in grouping in the binary number system and converting to decimal number system.
Materials: 4 Cards made as shown.
Time: 15 to 20 minutes.
Skills: Counting, abstraction, addition, grouping.
Additional Information: The students can be encouraged to create a Binary

Magic Game for numbers from 1 to 31. This would mean another card for the group of 16 and additions to the 4 cards shown.

Follow-Up: The game of "Nim" or "A Toss of the Dice."

Nim

Nim is an old English word meaning "take" or "steal." As a game, NIM is an old two-player game, possibly from the Chinese. You can play with pennies, bits of paper, even marbles. Arrange twelve items in three groups as shown:

XXX
XXXX
XXXXX

Here are the rules:

Players take turns removing one or more markers from any one of the three rows. The player who takes the last marker, WINS!

It would be nice to know how to play so that you would almost always win. You can, if you remember the binary number system. First, write the numbers of markers in any row as a binary number; then add the numbers.

XXX	011_2
XXXX	100_2
XXXXX	101_2
	212 (total)

In order to win, you should always look for the column or columns that add up to an odd number, and then take away enough markers to change the sum so that each column adds up to an even number.

In this case if you take only one marker from the top row,

XX	010_2
XXXX	100_2
XXXXX	101_2
	211 (total)

you have made matters worse. But if you take two markers from the top row,

X	001_2
XXXX	100_2
XXXXX	101_2
	202 (total)

everything is in order because the middle column is no longer an odd sum. Suppose that your opponent takes two from the bottom row:

X	001_2
XXXX	100_2
XXX	011_2
	112 (total)

You could take two markers from the middle row to get rid of the odd numbers in the total.

$$X \qquad 001_2$$
$$XX \qquad 010_2$$
$$XXX \qquad 011_2$$
$$22 \text{ (total)}$$

If your opponent takes one from the top row, what would you do?

$$XX \qquad 010_2$$
$$XXX \qquad 011_2$$

Of course, take one from the bottom row:

$$XX \qquad 010_2$$
$$XX \qquad 010_2$$
$$200 \text{ (total)}$$

Your opponent now takes one from the middle row. See if you can finish the game and WIN!

$$XX \qquad 010_2$$
$$X \qquad 001_2$$
$$11 \text{ (total)}$$

You can change the rules so that whoever takes the last marker loses. You can add many more markers on each row to make a very challenging game.

TEACHER'S CORNER
Purpose: Drill in converting to binary numbers.
Materials: 12 markers, rules of the game.
Time: 20-30 minutes—one run of the game probably takes 7 to 10 minutes.
Skills: Following directions, planning, addition, binary number conversion.
Follow-Up: "A Toss of the Dice" given as a homework problem make a nice follow-up and provides closure to this lesson.

A Toss of the Dice
A pair of dice, used in a board game, consists of two die. Each die is a cube, or six-sided figure, with the numbers one to six, one on each face of the die. It is fun to make your own dice for a board game. You are to make your dice with binary numbers on the faces. Use the binary numbers from 1 to 110 .

TEACHER'S CORNER
Purpose: This activity allows the student to work independently and to put into practice the concepts of binary numbers.
Materials: Cardboard to form the 2 cubes, magic markers. Alternatively real dice can be used and the faces can be covered with sticky labels.

Time: 30 minutes or less as a homework project.
Skills: Craft skill, following instructions, binary number conversion.
Follow-Up: The students should be encouraged to use their dice in a board game. The students might want to make a class board game based on computer terms or concepts.

The Power of the Penny

Many years ago in the country of India the Rajah wanted a new game. A countryman invented the game of chess for him. It so pleased the Rajah that he offered the man anything he wanted. "Wonderful," said the man, "please give me one grain of wheat (wheat was very important in India at that time) for the first square of the chess board, two grains for the second square and so forth." Figure it out. Perhaps you can get your parents to give you one penny on the first day of the month, two pennies on the second day, four pennies on the third day, and so on to the end of a month. Do you think they will agree?

TEACHER'S CORNER
Purpose: Practice in the concept of powers of two.
Time: Homework assignment.
Skill: Mathematics.
Additional Information: The teacher should realize that the students may not be able to come up with the final answer, which is $(2**30-1)$ or 1,073,741,823.

Table Talk
CAN YOU COMPLETE THIS TABLE?

All the numbers from one to fifteen are in the table. We have started to write down the binary representation for these numbers. We need your help to complete it.

TABLE

DECIMAL	BINARY
1	0001
2	0011
3	
4	
5	
6	
7	
8	
9	
10	
11	
12	
13	
14	
15	

TEACHER'S CORNER
Purpose: This is a reinforcing experience representing numbers in a base other than 10.
Materials: Above activity and chart, pencil.
Time: 10-15 minutes.
Skills: Abstraction, grouping, counting, place value.
Additional Information: This completed activity could be made into a poster or chart for the bulletin board. The poster would be helpful in introducing "Binary Magic" and "Nim" to the students.

ADDING NUMBERS
Here is a table to help you add two numbers:

	0	1	2	3	4	5	6	7	8	9
0	0	1	2	3	4	5	6	7	8	9
1	1	2	3	4	5	6	7	8	9	10
2	2	3	4	5	6	7	8	9	10	11
3										
4										
5										
6										
7										
8										
9										

To add 1 and 5, read across the row marked with a 1 until you find a column marked with a 5. The number in the box will be the answer to the sum 1 + 5. Complete this table.

TEACHER'S CORNER
Purpose: Lead-in activity to creating a binary addition table.
Materials: Teacher created worksheet.
Time: Homework or 15 to 30 minutes classtime.
Skills: Addition, use of a table.

ADDING BINARY NUMBERS
Here is a binary addition table. It is only partly filled. Can you fill in the rest?

	000	001	010	011	100
000					
001					
010	010	011	100	101	110
011					
100					

TEACHER'S CORNER
Purpose: Drill and practice with binary numbers system.
Materials: Teacher created worksheet.
Time: 30 minutes.
Skills: Abstraction, grouping, place value.

Gears and Gadgets
JUNKYARD
Take a trip to a local junkyard to get an odometer from an old car. Take it apart for a better look. Can you put it back together?

TEACHER'S CORNER
Purpose: To see how a gear counter works.
Time: Homework project.
Skill: Mechanical.
Additional Information: Parental cooperation is suggested for this project. An automobile mechanic from the community could be invited to the class to show how an odometer works.

YOU CAN COUNT ON IT
Use an abacus to do addition and subtraction. The abacus is a computing instrument used by the Chinese for generations. Each bead below the bar in an abacus counts 1, each one above the bar counts 5. Working from right to left, each column or rod on the abacus represents units, tens, hundreds, etc. You can operate the abacus with the right hand only. The thumb moves the first point bead upward, the index finger moves the first point bead downwards, the middle finger moves the fifth point bead up and down.

Addition: To add 123 + 123, set up the figure on the abacus as shown:

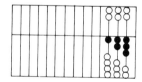

In the same column, repeat the operation

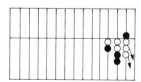

If you add another 123 to this figure your abacus will show 369.

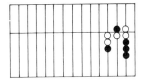

The calculation of each column is completed before the next is undertaken, when the five lower beads are against the bar, one five point bead is moved downwards and the five one point beads are moved back to their starting position. When both five point beads are down, a one point bead in the next left hand column is moved up and two five point beads are returned to their original position. It is not possible to have a reply showing both five point beads at the down position as this denotes "ten." Always start with the first column at your right and proceed to the next column.

Subtract: Subtraction is made from left to right. To subtract 76 from 93, set up 93 on the abacus:

Subtract 7 from the left column, raise one five point bead and lower two one point beads. In the right side column, subtract 6. As you cannot subtract six from three, borrow ten. Lower a one point bead in the left column (which leaves you only a one point bead in the tens column). In order to borrow ten in the left column, lower two five point beads in the upper right column. You now have beads of value 13 in the right column. Raise one five point bead and lower a one point bead which leaves you with one five point bead above and two one point beads below the bar, or seven. Your abacus now reads 17.

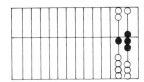

TEACHER'S CORNER
Purpose: To become familiar with one of the earliest computing devices.
Materials: Teacher created worksheet, abacus.
Time: 30 minutes.

Skills: Following directions, manual dexterity, counting, grouping by fives.
Additional Information: An abacus can be made using a cigar box, straws, and macaroni.

ALL GEARED UP

Make your own simple calculator. Use a bandsaw with a 1/2 inch blade. Cut three 3/4 inch thick pieces of plywood into circular disks. Each disk should be four inches in diameter. Stack the three disks together with two nails as shown:

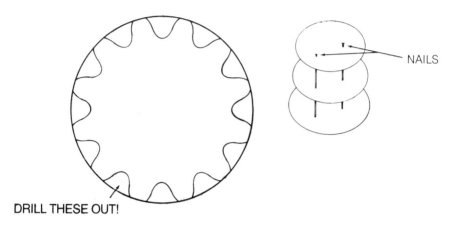

DRILL THESE OUT!

Now trace the pattern shown onto the top disk. Then drill out the pieces between each tooth in the diagram using a 1/4 inch drill. After you cut out the spaces between the teeth, smooth the grooves with sandpaper. Drill a 1/4 inch hole in the EXACT center of the stack of disks. Separate the pile being careful not to break the teeth. (One could varnish or lacquer the gears to protect the teeth.) Cut off all but one tooth on ONE gear. Press dowel sticks 1 and 1/2 inches long and 1/4 inch in diameter into the center holes in all the gears. These are the gear shafts. Now place these gears on a flat board about 10 inches by 12 inches. Follow the diagram to place the gears and number them as shown.

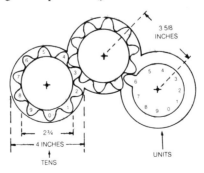

To add, turn the gears clockwise. For example to add 4 and 12, turn the ones gear four turns clockwise. To express adding 12, turn the ones gear twice and the tens gear once. Your calculator should read 16 (one ten and 6 ones or 16).

TEACHER'S CORNER
Purpose: To see how a gear counter works.
Materials: Teacher created worksheet, cardboard or plywood disks, sticks or dowels.
Time: Homework project.
Skills: Following instructions, building.
Additional Information: Parental guidance necessary.

RELATED READINGS

(**S** -Student, **T** -Teacher)

1. Adler, Irving. *Numbers Old and New.* Day, 1960. (**S,T**)
2. Butter, Ian. *Number Symbolism.* Rutledge, 1970 (**T**)
3. Epstein, Samuel. *First Book of Codes and Ciphers.* Watts, 1956. (**S**)
4. Goldstine, Herman Hine. *The Computer from Pascal to von Neumann.* Princeton University Press, 1973. (**T**)
5. Halacy, Daniel Stephen. *Charles Babbage, Father of the Computer.* Crowell-Collier Press, 1970. (**S**)
6. Harmon, Margaret. *Stretching Man's Mind; a History of Data Processing.* Mason, 1975. (**T**)
7. Kohn, Bernice. *Secret Codes and Ciphers.* Prentice Hall, 1968. (**S**)
8. Meadow, Charles. *Story of Computers.* Harvey, 1970. (**S**)
9. Mims, Forrest. *Number Machines; An Introduction to the Abacus Slide Rule, and Pocket Calculator.* Makay, 1977. (**S,T**)
10. Moseley, Maboth. *Irascible Genius; The Life of Charles Babbage.* H. Regnery Company, 1970. (**T**)
11. Randell, Brian. *The Origins of Digital Computers.* Springer-Verlag, 1973. (**T**)
12. Rosenberg, Jerry Martin. *The Computer Prophets.* MacMillian, 1969. (**T**)
13. Rusch, Richard. *Computers: Their History and How They Work.* Simon and Schuster, 1969. (**S**)
14. Sitomer, Mindel. *How Did Numbers Begin?* Thomas Y. Crowell Company, 1976. (**S,T**)
15. St. John, Glory. *How to Talk Like A Martian.* Walck, 1975. (**S,T**)
16. Turck, J.A.V. *Origin of Modern Calculating Machines.* Arno Press, 1972. (**T**)
17. Vorwald, Alan, Clard, Frank. *Computers: From Sand Table to Electric Brain.* McGraw-Hill Book Company, 1970. (**S,T**)
18. Watson, Clyde. *Binary Numbers.* Crowell, 1977. (**S,T**)

Chapter 4

How Do Computers Work?

THE COMPUTER AS A PROBLEM SOLVER

The purpose of this chapter is to acquaint the student with problem-solving techniques, the structure of a computer, and implementation of a problem solution on a computer. A typical programming language (TPL) will be used as the vehicle for showing how these concepts work together.

PARTS OF THE COMPUTER

Before we can understand how a computer can be used to solve problems, we must look at the physical and logical composition of the computer. This collection of computer components, called **hardware,** is made up of five parts: the **input device,** the **memory,** the **arithmetic unit,** the **output device,** and the **central processing unit** (Fig. 4.1).

The Input Device

When humans are given a problem to solve, they are told some facts pertaining to that problem. That is, they are given "input." The "devices" they use to accept this knowledge might be eyes, ears, and to a lesser extent other senses.

The computer also needs to be given information which is entered through an input device. This device might be a card reader which reads or scans the holes punched in a computer card. An input device might be a keyboard, like a typewriter, upon which we can type the information. The input device could be an optical scanner much like the scanners that read the Universal Product Code (UPC) on an item purchased at the grocery. An input device might be a hand-held light pen which sends signals to a cathode ray tube (CRT) screen (Fig. 4.2).

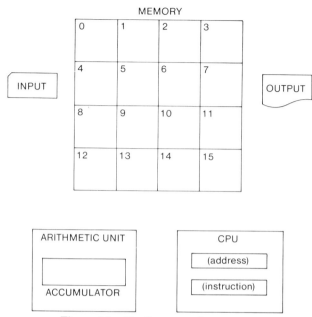

Figure 4.1   The five parts of a computer.

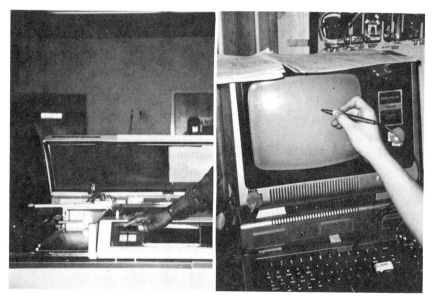

Figure 4.2   Typical input devices, a card reader and a light pen.   *Photo by S. Heller.*

The Memory Unit

When humans are asked to solve a problem, they are given some initial facts, but then they usually have to call upon their memory to remind them of facts or techniques they have learned. Sometimes the information stored in the memory portion of the brain is not enough to help solve the problem. Sometimes the information needed is not used often, so it hasn't been committed to memory. In such cases it is necessary to go to books, charts, and tables for the information.

In the same fashion the computer has a memory area where information is stored. The computer memory is like a set of electronic mailboxes, each with its own address. These mail boxes can hold data or program instructions for immediate use. The computer also has a secondary memory called peripheral storage which is used to house information that is needed, but not used often enough to be kept in the main memory.

The Arithmetic Unit

When humans begin to calculate the answer to the problem, "wheels spin in the brain," and they come up with the answer. The arithmetic unit of the computer is where basic mathematical calculations of addition and subtraction are performed. The results of these calculations are temporarily placed in a special part of the arithmetic unit called the **accumulator.**

The Output Device

When humans want to communicate information to each other, they can speak about it or write about it. The computer, too, uses devices for communicating information to a user. Such output devices are printers, screens, punched cards, and even voice synthesizers (Fig. 4.3).

The Central Processing Unit

The processes that allow humans to solve a problem are controlled by a part of the brain. The computer also has a director, a central processing unit (CPU), which controls the entire procedure and coordinates the interaction of the parts of a computer as they work together. In a **stored program computer**, the CPU reads and **executes** or carries out instructions stored in the memory. Instructions are executed one by one. As each instruction is executed, different parts of the computer are activated. If the instruction calls for input, the input device is activated; if a calculation has to be made, the arithmetic unit is readied.

A computer's five typical parts often appear to be in a physical arrangement of three pieces: an input/output unit, a central processing/arithmetic unit, and a memory unit. Figure 4.4 shows how information travels around within the computer. The diagram also shows how the central processing unit directs the control of a problem.

Figure 4.3   Typical output devices, a printer and a CRT screen.

Courtesy of Radio Shack, a division of Tandy Corp.

How is a computer used to solve a problem? A computer needs to be instructed in a language especially designed for the computer. How does a person prepare instructions in a computer language? The person needs to have a "plan of attack" before writing the computer language instructions. Trying to have a computer solve a problem without the plan of attack is like trying to bake a cake without a recipe.

PROBLEM-SOLVING TECHNIQUE

The first step in preparing a plan is to understand the problem completely. Sometimes there are ambiguities in the statement of the problem simply because the problem has been stated in human language. For example, a command to "draw the drapes" might cause one person to close the curtains and another person to sketch them. In preparing a problem solution, it is necessary first to carefully analyze the original description of the problem and to make sure that you understand exactly what is expected. In the problem *"Find the sum of all integers from 2 to 10 inclusive,"* we must make sure that we understand the terms sum, integer, and inclusive, in order to correctly answer the problem. (The correct answer would be $2+3+4+5+6+7+8+9+10 = 54$.)

The second step in problem-solving is to prepare a general outline of the tasks which must be completed to arrive at the solution. This outline should be a list of WHAT has to be done, not HOW to do it. For example, in the prob-

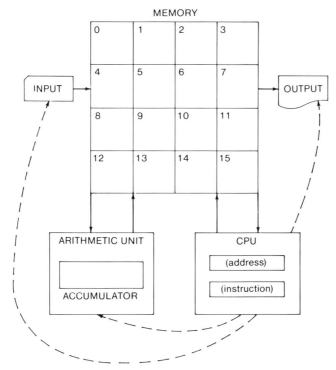

Figure 4.4 The five parts of the computer with solid lines to illustrate data flow and dotted lines to illustrate control flow.

lem: *"Use a telephone to find out the time from a recorded message,"* we could list the tasks as follows:

```
1. Determine the correct phone number.
2. Place the call.
```

One might be tempted to include in this list such things as handling a busy signal, listening to the recording, and hanging up the phone. These actions are specific details of HOW to accomplish the WHAT to do tasks we have outlined for the problem.

The third step in problem-solving is to refine these WHAT to do tasks into a detailed list of HOW to do it. In refining

```
1. Determine the correct phone number.
```

we could list the following steps:

```
1. If the phone number is not known
      then
         look it up in a phone book.
```

As you can see, we could refine this task further to deal with the situation in which there is no phone book.

Continuing to refine our outline, the next task

```
2. Place the call.
```

could be broken down as follows:

```
2a. Lift the receiver.
2b. Listen for the dial tone.
2c. ''Dial'' the number.
2d. If the telephone number is busy
        then
            hang up and repeat from 2a
        otherwise
            listen to the recorded message.
2e. Hang up.
```

Here one can see that even in this refinement, some detail is still missing. Looking at 2c, we have failed to say exactly HOW to "dial" the number. Once we have completely refined our problem, the detailed solution might look like this:

```
1. If the phone number is not known
        then
            if there is a phone book
        then
            look up the number
        otherwise
            call the information operator.
2.
    2a. Lift the receiver.
    2b. Listen for the dial tone.
    2c. If this phone has a dial
            then
                dial the number
            otherwise
                press the buttons.
    2d. If the number is busy
            then
                hang up and repeat from 2a.
            otherwise
                listen to recorded message.
    2e. Hang up.
```

FLOWCHARTS

A flowchart is a picture of a step-by-step solution. The symbols used to represent the possible actions to be taken are shown in figure 4.5.

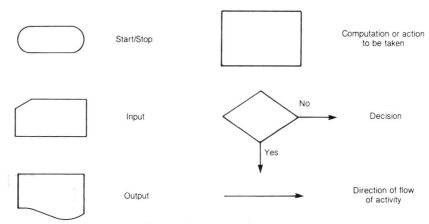

Figure 4.5 Flowchart symbols.

Figure 4.6 is a flowchart of the solution of the problem: *"Use the telephone to find out the time from a recorded message."*

When introducing this step-by-step approach in problem solving to your students, it is important that you begin with an example that is relevant to their experience and one that allows their active participation. For example, you might ask the students to give the directions for making chocolate milk. You should establish for the children what ingredients and utensils are available (i.e., chocolate powder, spoon, milk, glass, pan to catch the spills). After they have developed their directions, you will have to demonstrate the results of following EXACTLY their rules. Exaggeration may help you illustrate the consequences of imprecise directions. For example, overflowing the glass or leaving the spoon in the glass might produce hilarious results.

This same technique of problem-solving by refinement is even more appropriate for developing the solution of mathematical problems. If we were presented with the task of finding the area of a rectangle whose length is 10 centimeters and whose width is 5 centimeters, we could outline the solution of the problem as follows:

```
1. Find the area.
2. Present the area.
```

In refining the outline we could give the HOW TO solution as

```
1. Area is equal to 10 x 5.
2. Write the value of the area
      on the blackboard.
```

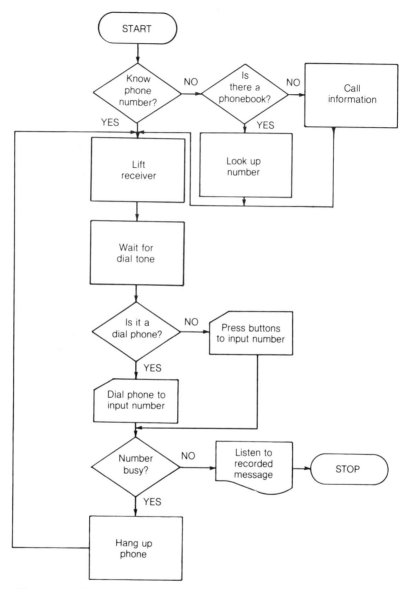

Figure 4.6 Using the telephone to find out the time from a recorded message.

Fortunately, we can get an immediate answer because we know the actual value of the sides of the rectangle. Suppose we were asked to find the area of a rectangle whose length and width measurements would be told to us at a later time. We could still prepare the solution steps. Not having the actual numbers doesn't prevent us from outlining the solution. The initial WHAT to do outline could be as follows:

```
1. Determine the measurement of
      the length & width.
2. Calculate the area.
3. Present the answer (the value
      of the area).
```

When refining our solution for use on a computer, we can represent these unknown quantities by **variables.** For example, we can represent the measurement of the side of the rectangle by variables which we can call LENGTH and WIDTH. Similarly we can represent the area calculated by the variable AREA.

Now our outline looks like this:

```
1. Input the LENGTH and WIDTH  value.
2. Calculate  AREA = LENGTH x WIDTH.
3. Output AREA value.
```

Realistically, we would not go to all this effort to calculate the area for only one rectangle at one time. We would want to prepare the solution for the general problem to find the area for each rectangle in a group of rectangles. How are we actually going to perform these calculations? Clearly we are not going to enumerate each rectangle and its dimensions. We want to set up a process which we can repeat as often as necessary to complete the calculations for the set of rectangles. Such a process is called a **loop.** Our outline would then look like this:

```
1. While there is another rectangle whose area is
      to be calculated
   repeat
   1a. Determine the input.
   1b. Calculate the area.
   1c. Present the answer.
2. Stop.
```

And refining the outline:

```
1. While there is another rectangle
      whose area is to be calculated
   repeat
   1a. Input LENGTH and WIDTH value.
   1b. Calculate AREA = LENGTH x WIDTH.
   1c. Output AREA value.
2. Stop.
```

Figure 4.7 is a flowchart for the solution of the problem: *"Find the area of a set of rectangles."*

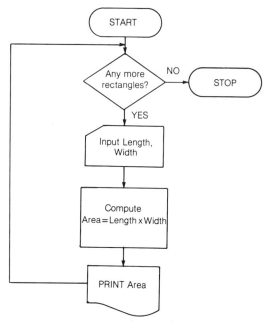

Figure 4.7   Finding the area of a set of rectangles.

Sometimes we encounter problems which require us to count the number of times we repeat an action. This type of loop is illustrated in the following example: *Produce and print a countdown from 10 to 1 and then output the word BLASTOFF."* The step by step solution might look like this:

```
1. Determine the input.
2. Count down and print.
3. Present the answer.
```

Looking at step number 1, "Determine the input," we realize that this problem gives us all the necessary information. There is no need to accept input, but we need to state the point at which we will begin the countdown. So we can rephrase step number one:

```
1. Start the count at 10.
```

The refinement of step 2 requires a loop. We want to repeat step 2 until we reach the BLASTOFF signal. Refinement of step 2 is then:

```
2. While COUNT is greater than zero
   repeat
   2a. Print current COUNT value
   2b. Reduce the value of COUNT by 1.
```

In order to insure that we count backwards from 10, we must include the instruction to reduce the COUNT value. Finishing this step-by-step refinement, "Present the answer" becomes:

```
3. Print ''BLASTOFF.''
4. Stop.
```

The complete solution is as follows:

```
1. Start the COUNT at 10.
2. While the COUNT is greater than zero
   repeat
   2a. Print COUNT value
   2b. Reduce COUNT value by 1.
3. Print ''BLASTOFF.''
4. Stop.
```

You might want to try to rewrite this step-by-step solution to produce a countup to BLASTOFF starting at 1 and ending at 10. This simple solution provides you with a basic structure for any problem that requires a counted loop starting and ending at given values. Figure 4.8 is a flowchart for the solution of the problem: *"Produce and print the countdown from 10 to 1 and output "BLASTOFF."''*

The problem-solving outlines that we have illustrated are part of a process called algorithmic development. An **algorithm** , as we can see, is like a recipe for solving a problem. It is a way of organizing a problem into small, definite steps so that it can be translated into a programming language and used on the computer. An algorithm must be specific enough so there is no ambiguity, finite so there is a definitive stopping place in the process, and general enough to handle a group of cases. An algorithm usually has input information and MUST include a step for outputting or presenting the answer.

You will notice that many of the activities appropriate for this section could be tied to other areas in your current curriculum. The skill of being able to create a step-by-step plan of action is being emphasized in all subject areas. The activities also use verbalization, language skills, writing skills, and map reading skills, as well as math skills. For example, the activity, "The Tour Guide," could easily be incorporated into a map lesson, a lesson about your

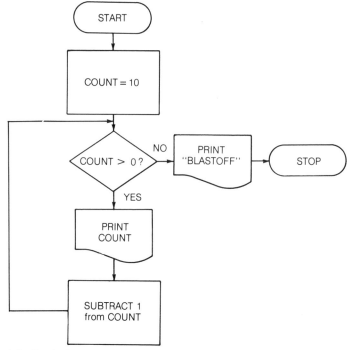

Figure 4.8 Producing and printing a countdown sequence terminated by "BLAST-OFF."

community's history, or a community workers lesson. Children might have the tour guide "stop" at certain landmarks and give pertinent information about the history of the landmark or the jobs of the workers there.

PROGRAMMING THE SOLUTION

Now that we have examined the step-by-step technique for preparing the solution for a problem, we need to put that solution into a set of steps that the computer can understand. This set of steps is called a **programming language** and the final version of our problem solution in such a language is called a **program.** Our program represents the problem to be solved. The program is called the **software** that controls the hardware of the computer.

Some programming languages are tailored to the hardware of the computer and are called **assembly languages** or machine languages. There are also high-level, **problem-oriented languages** such as FORTRAN, BASIC, Pascal or COBOL which are available on many computers.

We will use the example of the area of a rectangle to demonstrate a program in assembly language as well as in a high-level language. The assembly language we will use is an imaginary one, TPL. TPL, Typical Programming

Language, will illustrate the flow of control through the computer. The high-level language we will use is a real one, BASIC. BASIC will illustrate what an actual program looks like. We will not attempt to teach any programming language in this book. There are many good introductory texts for each of the programming languages.

In order to use TPL to solve the area of a rectangle problem, we first need to know what commands are available to us. These commands are listed in Table 4.1. In all of the commands, "a" represents an address or a location in memory.

TPL COMMAND SET:

READ	a –	input command which will read data into memory location "a" from an input device (i.e. READ 15 means read data into memory location 15).
PRINT	a –	command which will send data from memory location "a" to the output device.
LOAD	a –	loads information from memory location "a" into the accumulator in the arithmetic unit.
STORE	a –	stores information from the accumulator into memory location "a."
ADD	a –	adds information in memory location "a" to the value in the accumulator.
SUB	a –	subtracts information in memory location "a" from the value in the accumulator.
MUL	a –	multiplies information in the accumulator by the value in memory location "a."
DIV	a –	divides information in the accumulator by the value in memory location "a."
STOP	–	terminates the program.

Table 4.1 The TPL Command Set.

To create the TPL program we must go to the last outline of our solution and write the TPL commands which will accomplish that outline. To input length and width of the rectangle, we must READ into two memory locations. (Since there must be room in our imaginary 16-word memory for the program to be stored, we have chosen to start reading the data into locations 12 and 13 in order not to place values on top of the program instructions.) To calculate the area, we must first LOAD one value, in location 12, into the accumulator. Then MUL the accumulator by the second value, in location 13. (All arithmetic operations must take place in the arithmetic unit, with the result placed in the accumulator, one at a time.) In order to find out what the final product or area is, we must STORE the result back into memory. From there it can be output with a PRINT command. The TPL program is shown in Table 4.2:

Algorithm	TPL	
1. Input length and	READ	12
width values	READ	13
2. Calculate Area=length	LOAD	12
times width	MUL	13
	STORE	14
3. Output length, width	PRINT	12
and area values	PRINT	13
	PRINT	14
4. Stop	STOP	

Table 4.2   The TPL program.

In order to understand how the program is run on the computer, you must first visualize a deck of input cards. The program part of the input has one command per line (Fig. 4.9). This is followed by two lines of data, with the values for length (30) and width (20). The program must first be loaded into the computer memory where it will sit waiting to be carried out or executed.

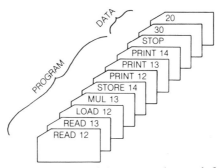

Figure 4.9   A TPL program and data prepared on cards for execution.

Figure 4.10 depicts the program loaded into memory with the two data values still waiting in the input device.

When the CPU receives the signal to **execute** (carry out) the program, it will start at location 0. It will examine one command at a time and cause it to be carried out. When it encounters READ 12, it will activate the input device and cause data, the number 30, to be read into memory location 12 (Fig. 4.11).

Similarly, READ 13 will cause the data, the number 20, to be read into location 13 (Fig. 4.12).

LOAD 12 will cause the number 30 to be loaded into the accumulator (Fig. 4.13).

MUL 13 will cause the value 30 (in the accumulator) to be multiplied by the value 20 (in location 13), and the result of 600 will be in the accumulator (Fig. 4.14).

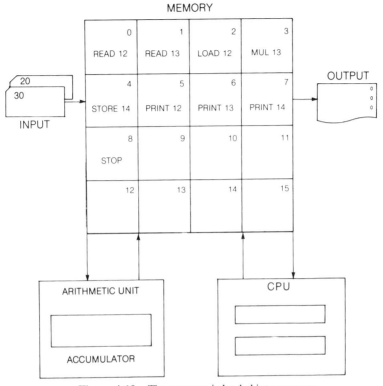

MEMORY

	0	1	2	3
	READ 12	READ 13	LOAD 12	MUL 13

OUTPUT

INPUT

20
30

	4	5	6	7
	STORE 14	PRINT 12	PRINT 13	PRINT 14

	8	9	10	11
	STOP			

	12	13	14	15

ARITHMETIC UNIT

ACCUMULATOR

CPU

Figure 4.10   The program is loaded into memory.

STORE 14 will cause the result 600 to be put into location 14 in memory (Fig. 4.15).

The three successive PRINTs will send 30, 20 and 600 to the output device (Fig. 4.16).

After execution of the program, our imaginary computer will look like Figure 4.17.

Assembly language programming, such as TPL, requires a detailed knowledge of the hardware of the particular computer you are using. It is often preferable to use a high-level language which is compatible with many different computers. This eliminates much of the detail for the programmmer. A high-level language allows you to go from algorithm to program with greater ease. You should be aware that when you use a high-level language, it must go through a translation process called compiling. A **compiler** is software that converts the high-level language program into the machine language of the particular computer. This compiling process takes place without any effort on the part of the programmer. It is similar to giving a speech in English at the United Nations and having it translated into several languages by interpreters while you

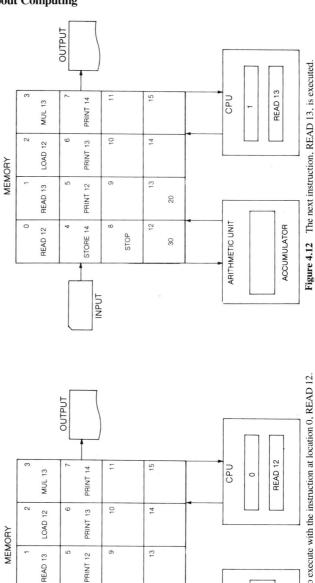

Figure 4.12   The next instruction, READ 13, is executed.

Figure 4.11   The program starts to execute with the instruction at location 0, READ 12.

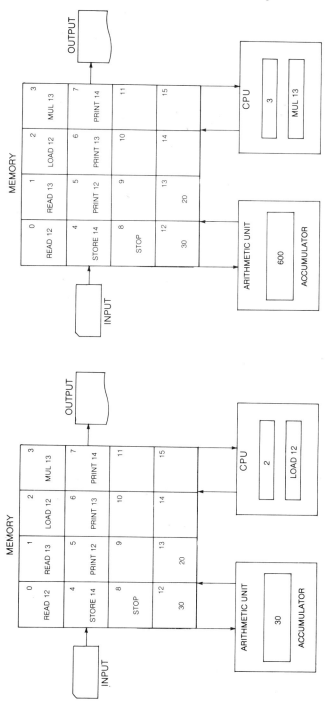

Figure 4.14   The value in the accumulator is multiplied by the value 20 from location 13 for a result of 600 in the accumulator.

Figure 4.13   The LOAD 12 causes the value 30 in location 12 to be loaded into the accumulator.

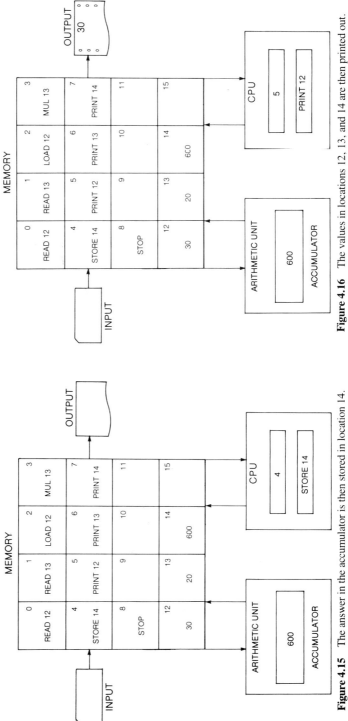

Figure 4.16   The values in locations 12, 13, and 14 are then printed out.

Figure 4.15   The answer in the accumulator is then stored in location 14.

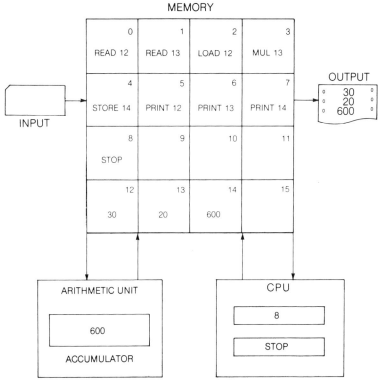

Figure 4.17   The final result when the program comes to a STOP.

are speaking. The compiler "interprets" the high-level language, such as BASIC, for the computer. As you can see in the BASIC example in Table 4.3, with a high-level language you don't have to be concerned with the memory locations or with loading into or storing from the accumulator. These details are taken care of by the high-level language itself. (The BASIC commands have numbers in front of each one which cause the computer to save the commands in memory in numerical order.)

Algorithm:	BASIC:
1. Input length and and width	10 INPUT L, W
2. Calculate area=length times width	20 LET A= L*W
3. Output length,width and area	30 PRINT L, W, A
4. Stop	40 END

Table 4.3 A BASIC Program.

DATA ORGANIZATION

In addition to understanding the computer hardware and the computer software, it is also important to consider the **data** that will be worked on by the hardware and software. In our previous examples we were dealing with simple numbers for data. However, frequently we are asked to solve problems involving alphabetic information (input a list in alphabetical order), or a combination of alphabetic (names, addresses) and numeric (charge account) information. Often a significant part of problem solving is deciding how to organize the information before trying to write a program to work on the data. A good exercise for students is to have them practice putting information into some logical order in tables as in the example below (Table 4.4).

CLASS INTEREST DATA BASE

NAME	AGE	SEX	MONTH of BIRTH	HOBBY	FAVORITE FOOD
Jenny	11	F	Jan	horses	pizza
Chuckie	9	M	Feb	crafts	pizza
Adam	11	M	May	soccer	pizza
Matt	8	M	June	games	pizza
Josh	14	M	May	computers	pizza

Table 4.4   A sample data base.

Information that is organized in this logical fashion is called a **file.** When you have many files put together, such a collection of data is called a **data base.**

DOCUMENTATION

The final aspect of writing programs to solve problems on the computer is that of good **documentation.** By documentation we mean a description of the problem as well as the description of the solution or algorithm for the problem. Documentation should also include a description of the input and expected output for the problem. It is important to emphasize good documentation as a necessary step in the whole problem solving process. The preparation of good documentation is an especially valuable experience for any student who hopes to have a career in the computer field someday.

KEY IDEAS

Hardware
Input Device
Output Device
Memory
Central Processing Unit
Arithmetic Unit
Accumulator
Stored Program Computer
Algorithm
Flowchart
Variable
Loop
Assembly Language
Problem-Oriented Language
Software
Program
Programming Language
Execute
Compiler
Data
File
Data Base
Documentation

ACTIVITIES

Computer Vocabulary Builders
BE YOUR OWN WEBSTER
Prepare a computer dictionary, listing in alphabetical order the parts of a computer. Define these parts.

TEACHER'S CORNER
Purpose: Vocabulary building activity.
Materials: Teacher created worksheet.
Time: 15-30 minutes.
Skills: Alphabetizing, dictionary skills.

Additional Information: The teacher may want to combine all of the vocabulary building activities (A-D) into a set of learning centers, allowing students to choose several to do.

QUESTIONS PLEASE?

Here is a list of computer terms. Make up questions for these "answers."
INPUT
OUTPUT
CPU
ARITHMETIC UNIT
MEMORY
LOGICAL UNIT
COMPUTER
PROGRAM
ALGORITHM

TEACHER'S CORNER
Purpose: Vocabulary building activity.
Materials: Teacher created worksheet.
Time: 15-30 minutes.
Skills: Vocabulary, dictionary, inductive reasoning.

COMPUTER GIGO
You can use the questions you made in activity B to play a GIGO game. Make game cards with the computer terms on them. One student will ask the question and those students who have the "answer" on their card can mark it. The first student to complete his or her card, WINS! Example of a GIGO card:

INPUT	CPU	MEMORY
LOGICAL UNIT	FREE	PROGRAM
OUTPUT	COMPUTER	ALGORITHM

TEACHER'S CORNER
Purpose: Vocabulary building activity.
Materials: Teacher created worksheet, posterboard or 5x7 index cards, markers.
Time: 30 minutes to make the game, 30 minutes to play the game.
Skills: Vocabulary, recall.

WORD-FIND

Here is a rectangle filled with hidden words. Can you find 11 computer words?

```
A P S R I N P U T R I N P U
R M A S L N A V W C X C D B
I N L O G I C A L U N I T R
T R G L O B T U W B X B E A
H T O O R S D R Y R O L F T
M O R E F C R A Z U A G N N
E I I F C H Q A T T H P Z I
T M T Y O I P P O A Y B F A
I A H P M J U K N A A U X E
C O M P U T E R J R B W A Z
U T O R P T O K M C Q C B D
N E P I T L U S L P D A R A
I R R N E V X C Y U G R E C
T M O C R N M I R E Q S M F
A I G E E O R Y O O M P E E
F N R I C E P N M O H G F G
S A A O D G H C E R R F I Z
T L M A C A D E M Y A H S I
T E M P H I J H S N O T U X
I N O Y Z I U C G D T A H Z
F T P T J K E L M K U X L Z
```

Words to be found: logical unit, computer, arithmetic unit, memory, input, CPU, output, terminal, program, algorithm.

TEACHER'S CORNER
Purpose: Vocabulary-building activity.
Materials: Teacher created worksheet.
Time: 15-30 minutes.
Skills: Spelling, pattern recognition, review of vocabulary.

Problem-Solving Skills
BE A ROBOT

Pretend that you are a robot. You are only able to do EXACTLY as you are told. Have your classmates give you commands that will get you from your seat to the door.

TEACHER'S CORNER
Purpose: To introduce the step-by-step approach in problem solving to your students. It is important that you begin with an example that is relevant to their experience and one that allows their active participation.
Materials: Paper and pencil, student willing to be a robot.
Time: 15-20 minutes.
Skills: Logical thinking, sequencing, written expression.
Additional Information: After students have developed their directions, you will have to demonstrate the results of following their rules EXACTLY. Exaggeration may help you illustrate the consequences of imprecise directions. Do not let the limited writing skills of students keep them from expressing their rules. Do not count spelling!
Follow-Up: This is a preparation activity for the "Sticky Problem."

A STICKY PROBLEM
    Make a step-by-step solution for making a peanut butter and jelly sandwich using a loaf of bread, a jar of peanut butter, a jar of jelly and a knife. Exchange your solutions with your classmates and follow the instructions EXACTLY.

TEACHER'S CORNER
Purpose: To reinforce the step-by-step approach to problem solving.
Materials: A jar of peanut butter, a jar of jelly, one knife, a loaf of bread, table-top protector such as newspapers, paper towels or wax paper.
Time: 30-40 minutes depending on how many student solutions you wish to read and follow. Older students tend to take longer as they write in more detail.
Skills: Logical thinking, sequencing, writing.
Additional Information: Do not let the student's limited writing skills keep them from expressing the rules. Do not count spelling!
Follow-Up: Prepare, with the entire class, a "perfect" peanut butter and jelly sandwich solution. This could be put on a class bulletin board. A suggested homework follow-up is "Martian Maneuvers."

MARTIAN MANEUVERS
    Here is a map of outer space showing a Martian scout ship trying to return to home base, MARS.
    Use the four Martian words defined below to write a step-by-step solution so that the Martian scout ship can return safely to its base.

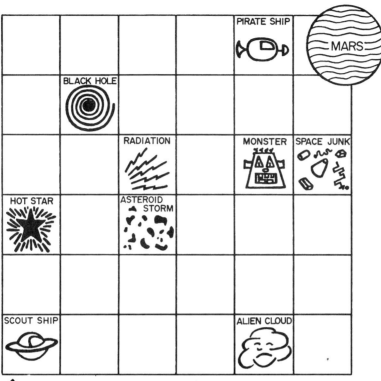

START   MARTIAN MANEUVERS

To move 1 block to the right, you say
   PARSEC in Martian.
To move one block to the left, you say
   WQRP in Martian.
To move one block up, you say
   TREW in Martian.
To move one block down, you say
   GORTP in Martian.

TEACHER'S CORNER

Purpose: This is a preprogramming activity designed to teach the student to prepare a step-by-step solution using a limited command set.
Materials: A teacher created worksheet of the above activity.
Time: 15-20 minutes (homework).
Skills: Logical thinking, sequencing, symbolic abstraction.

TOUR GUIDE

Prepare a step-by-step solution to guide a stranger to your town around the community, visiting five important places. (You can choose the five to visit. They might include the library, town government building, fire department, park, and the police station.)

TEACHER'S CORNER

Purpose: This is a problem-solving activity to help the student learn to express problems in a step-by-step solution.

Materials: Poster paper, map of town, magic markers.

Time: 30-45 minutes.

Skills: Map reading, sequencing, logical thinking.

TO SOLVE OR NOT TO SOLVE

In order for a problem to be solvable, it must be stated in a very clear way. Here is a list of problems. Mark those that are clearly stated.

1. Count the stars.
2. Count the number of windows in your home.
3. Buy comic books.
4. Buy three granola bars.
5. Dress yourself.
6. Put one pair of socks on your bare feet.
7. Give detailed directions from your front door to your school (by car, bus, or foot).

TEACHER'S CORNER

Purpose: This activity will help the students focus on the issue of which problems are solvable in a concrete way and which ones are not. This will be reemphasized when the students try to decide which problems are solvable on a computer.

Materials: Teacher created worksheet.

Time: 15-30 minutes.

Skills: Logical thinking.

Follow-Up: The exercise "Beyond Solution" is a good enrichment activity to follow this one. The teacher can also suggest that the students choose one of the solvable problems and draw a picture-chart describing its step-by-step solution.

BEYOND SOLUTION

Look at those problems that you did not mark. Try to write them in a different way so that they are clear and can be solved. For example, in the first one, "Count the stars," we are asking the impossible today. Scientists argue about where the universe ends. It would be better to ask for the solution to "Count the stars in the big dipper." Can you make this even more clear?

TEACHER'S CORNER
Purpose: To expand the concept of solvable problems.
Materials: Teacher created worksheet.
Time: 30 minutes.
Skills: Logical thinking, setting limits, being precise.

GO WITH THE FLOW
  The flowchart shown below is out of sequence. When it is in proper order it could be used to solve the problem "What to wear outside today?" Cut out the shapes of the flowchart and rearrange them to properly solve the problem.

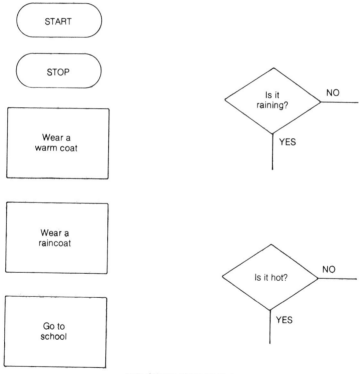

GO WITH THE FLOW

TEACHER'S CORNER
Purpose: To practice flowcharting solutions.
Materials: A teacher created worksheet of the flowchart, scissors, paste.
Time: 15 minutes.

Skills: Sequencing, logical thinking.
Additional Information: "Know How" would be a good follow up problem.

MORE GO WITH THE FLOW

Here is a flowchart. Follow it through and tell the class what the problem is that is being solved.

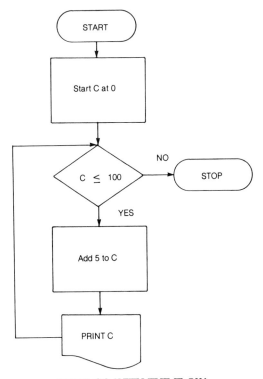

MORE GO WITH THE FLOW

TEACHER'S CORNER
Purpose: To practice following the logic of a flowchart.
Materials: Teacher created worksheet.
Time: 10 minutes.
Skill: Logical thinking.

KNOW HOW

Here are some problems that are clearly written. Pick one and prepare a step-by-step solution for the problem.

1. Give directions to get from your front door to your
    school in the morning, either by foot, car, or bus.

2. Take a science fiction book out of the public
   library nearest your home.
3. Play the game of Hangman with a friend.

TEACHER'S CORNER

Purpose: A preprogramming activity which reinforces the concept of step-by-step problem solution with familiar problems from daily life.
Materials: Teacher created worksheet, pencil.
Time: 30 minutes.
Skills: Logical thinking, precision, sequencing.
Additional Information: Suggest that your students flowchart the solution.
Follow-Up: It is suggested that the activity be used as a lead-in to the solution of numeric problems in the activity "Number Know How."

NUMBER KNOW HOW

   Here are some number problems. Choose one and write a step-by-step solution for the problem. Remember, no answer is needed. You are only telling HOW to get the answer.

1. Show how to find the area of a rectangle.
2. Show how to give the 5's multiplication table
   for 5 times 1 to 5 times 12 inclusive.
3. Get a grocery tape. Show how to add all the
   numbers on the tape.
4. Show how to decide how much change you would
   give a person who gave you a five dollar bill
   for a $3.72 item.

TEACHER'S CORNER

Purpose: To apply the step-by-step problem-solving techniques to numerical problems that are solvable.
Materials: Teacher created worksheet.
Time: 15-30 minutes.
Skills: Logical thinking, abstract reasoning, sequencing, precision.
Additional Information: The teacher can reinforce this activity by having teams of students produce flowchart pictures of the correct solution to hang on the bulletin board.

IT'S YOUR TURN

   Here is a step-by-step solution for a party game. Can you write the TPL (Typical Programming Language) for this solution?

1. Read date and month of birth as one
      number (for example, July 10th is 107).
2. Read age at last birthday.
3. Multiply date and month by 2.
4. Add 5 to answer in #3.
5. Multiply result in #4 by 50.
6. Add age at last birthday to answer
      in #5.
7. Add 365 to the results in #6.
8. Subtract 615 from answer in #7.
9. Write out the result in #8.

Your answer will be one number which is the day and month of your birthday and your current age.

TEACHER'S CORNER

Purpose: To reinforce the algorithm approach to problem solving.
Materials: Teacher created worksheet.
Time: 30 minutes to develop and try it out on several students.
Skills: Logical thinking, abstract reasoning, basic math facts of addition, subtraction, and multiplication.
Additional Information: This activity is the most formal problem-solving activity suggested so far. Because it can be solved on the computer, it is a good programming problem to use at a later time when programming skills are being developed. It is also a good problem to flowchart.

COMPUTER WORKS
   Play the computer simulation game to see how the parts of a computer work.

TEACHER'S CORNER

Description: This classroom game simulates how the different parts of the computer work. First instruct the children about the different parts of the computer (input, output, CPU, memory, arithmetic unit), and then assign these parts to them to act out. Every child can participate, since memory can be portrayed by one child or many children, each representing one memory cell. The teacher can make posterboard labels to identify each part:

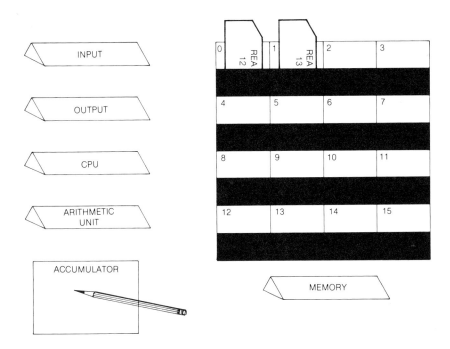

Explain the set of commands in a computer language called TPL (Typical Programming Language, see Table 4.1): Develop a simple program on the blackboard to read in two numbers, add them together, and print the answer:

READ   12
READ   13
LOAD   12
ADD   13
STORE   14
PRINT   12
PRINT   13
PRINT   14
STOP

DATA: 20, 14

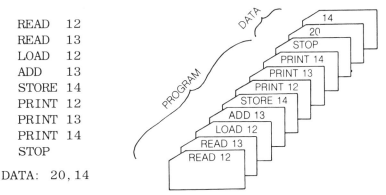

Once the program and data (two numbers) have been developed, put each command and data number on a separate posterboard card with magic markers.

Now the "director" (CPU) takes charge and tells the computer parts (students) what to do. The CPU commands the input device to read in the program cards (this is called loading the program into memory) into consecutive memory locations. Memory location 1 will have READ 12, memory location 2 will have READ 13, etc. After the program is loaded into memory, the CPU then looks at the commands one at a time, starting at location 1, and causes them to be carried out (executed). A READ 12 command from the CPU activates the input device to give a data card to memory location 12; a READ 13 command from the CPU activates the input device to give a data card to memory location 13. The LOAD 12 command causes the data in memory location 12 to be sent to the arithmetic unit. The ADD 13 causes the data in memory location 13 to be added to the information in the arithmetic unit. The STORE 14 causes the answer from the arithmetic unit to be put into memory location 14. The PRINT commands cause information to be sent to the output device.

Purpose: This activity is designed to show children how the parts of a computer interact.

Materials: Posterboard, paper to make labels and program cards.

Time: 40-45 minutes to develop the program and simulate the running of the program through the computer.

Skills: Verbal, following instructions, sequencing, problem solving.

Follow-Up: The teacher can choose to develop other problems in TPL. One possible problem would be finding the area of a rectangle given the length and width as input. The same simulation could be used to run this program. The students can be given the assignment of writing a TPL program for homework. The "It's Your Turn" activity describes another possible programming activity.

COMPUTER ANTICS

Below is a BASIC program to make the computer "laugh." Turn on the computer and type in:

```
10 PRINT "HA HA" (enter)
```

Now type:

```
RUN (enter)
```

Can you change the program to make the computer "cry."

Now look at this BASIC program to make the computer keep laughing. Type in:

```
10 PRINT "HA HA" (enter)
20 GO TO 10 (enter)
```

Now type:

```
RUN (enter)
```

To stop the laughing you will have to hit the BREAK key. Can you change the program to make the computer keep crying? You can use this program to make the computer repeat any sentence you want repeated.

TEACHER'S CORNER

Purpose: To provide a first experience in actually entering commands into a computer and observing the outcome.

Materials: A computer which has a BASIC language capability, teacher created worksheet.

Time: 10-15 minutes per student at the computer.

Skills: Reading, following instructions.

Additional Information: Young students are slow typists! Students might be more comfortable working in teams.

RELATED READINGS

(**S** -Student, **T** -Teacher)

1. Ball, Marion. *What Is A Computer?* Houghton Mifflin Company, 1972. (**S**)
2. Ball, Marion, and Charp, Sylvia. *Be A Computer Literate.* Creative Computing, 1978. (**S**)
3. Berger, Melvin. *Computers.* Coward, McCann and Geoghegan, 1972. (**S**)
4. Boy Scouts of America Merit Badge Series. *Computers.* Eastern Distribution Center, Charlotte, N.C. (**S**)
5. Brande, Michael. *Larry Learns About Computers.* T.S. Denison and Company. (**S**)
6. Brown, Richard. *Computers.* Viking Press, 1976. (**S**)
7. Chambers, Murray. *Computers and Young Children.* John Wiley and Sons, 1972. (**S**)
8. De Rossi, Claude. *Computers: Tools for Today.* Children's Press, 1972. (**S**)
9. Foley, Jacobs, Bower, and Basten. *Discovery and Structure: Individualizing Mathematics-Flowchart I, II, III.* Addison Wesley Publishing Co., 1970. (**S,T**)
10. Halacy, Daniel. *What Makes A Computer Work.* Little Brown & Company, 1973. (**S**)
11. Johanneson, Olaf. *The Tale of the Big Computer: A Vision.* Coward, McCann & Geoghegan, 1968. (**S**)
12. Jones, Weyman. *Computer: The Mind Stretcher.* Dial Press, 1969. (**S,T**)
13. Kinsler, Doris and Kinsler, Stephen. *Computers & Machines with a Memory.* Hawthorn Books, 1968. (**S**)
14. Kohn, Bernice. *Computers at Your Service.* Prentice-Hall 1966. (**S**)
15. Lawson, Harold. *Understanding Computer Systems.* Computer Science Press, 1982. (**T**)

16. Lewis, Bruce. *Meet The Computer.* Dodd, Mead & Company, 1977. (**S**)
17. Meadow, Charles. *The Story of Computers.* Harvey, 1970. (**S**)
18. O'Brien, Linda. *Computers.* Franklin Watts, 1978. (**S**)
19. Rice, Jean. *My Friend the Computer.* T.S.Denison & Company, 1976. (**S**)
20. Snyder, Gerald. *Let's Talk About Computers.* Jonathan David Publishers, 1973. (**S**)
21. Spencer, Donald. *Story of Computers.* Camelot, 1977. (**S,T**)
22. Spencer, Donald. *Computers in Action: How Computers Work.* Hayden Book Co., 1974. (**S,T**)
23. Srivastava, Jane. *Computers.* Coward, McCann & Geoghegan, 1972. (**S,T**)
24. Steinberg, Fred. *Computers.* Franklin Watts, 1969. (**S,T**)

Chapter 5

What Do Computers Do for Us?

COMPUTER APPLICATIONS

There is hardly an area in our lives that is not affected in some way by computers. In fact computers are so pervasive in our American way of life that we have all become **users** of computers in some way. The purpose of this unit is to create awareness of the computer impact in daily living. As users of computers it is important to understand that any computer application is only as good as the data and the program put into the system. The popular phrase, "Garbage In, Garbage Out (**GIGO**)," refers to that concept.

It is important to be able to identify **real-time** computer applications. A real-time system is one in which the results of calculations on incoming data influence the process being controlled immediately, rather than at some other time. An example would be the computer system that controls the space launches. Based on continuously arriving radar data describing the trajectory of the vehicle, adjustments are made to change that trajectory to keep the vehicle on the flight path.

Descriptions of many computer applications can be found in articles in current magazines and newspapers. The following outline of computer applications can be used for class discussion. The asterisk (*) denotes applications that can be found in most local communities.

Business

It is in the area of business data processing that computers first became widely used, starting in the early 1950's. In many of the categories described below, there is almost a complete dependence on the computer, particularly by large companies.

*1. Payroll processing: The computer is able to keep track of health bene-
fits, withholding taxes, employee stock plans, overtime, issuing of
checks, and all the other aspects of keeping a payroll.

*2. Personnel files: Employee records are routinely saved and manipulated
by the computer.

*3. Accounting, bookkeeping and auditing.

*4. Customer billing.

*5. Inventory control.

*6. **Point of sale marketing:**   The computerized checkout systems at many
grocery stores are a familar sight for most people (Fig. 5.1). The computer is able to store the current price of an item based upon its UPC, the
10-digit Universal Product Code adopted by the grocery industry. (The
UPC is usually printed somewhere on prepackaged items in the form of
vertical bars which identify the item and its manufacturer.) All aspects of
checkout can be handled by such a system, including keeping track of
taxable items, subtracting coupons, check-cashing identification, and
computing change due to the customer. More sophisticated systems also
provide a direct link between merchandise sale and inventory control.

7. Production Control: Computers are used to control processes in
manufacturing plants and industrial facilities. Entire segments of the automobile assembly lines are now computerized (Fig. 5.2). Oil refineries
and steel mills are monitored by computer. Quality control in the
manufacture of drugs (weight, count per bottle, etc.) is greatly automated.

8. **Management Information Systems (MIS):**   A huge amount of business
information is organized into a **data base.** This information can be retrieved and analyzed in many ways to aid management in decision-
making about sales, inventory, new plants and equipment, production,
market analysis, and advertising.

9. **Word Processing:**   This is a technique for typing information into a
memory unit on a typewriter or computer and then doing all the format-
ting and editing of that information at the keyboard (Fig. 5.3). In many
businesses, word processors have replaced the ordinary typewriter because they eliminate the retyping of drafts and save tremendous amounts
of time and paper. Form letters can also be saved and then called out of
memory to be duplicated and addressed to the recipients.

Finance

1. Stock exchange: AMCODE (American Stock Exchange Computerized
Order Display and Execution System) registers and executes all buy and

Figure 5.1 Point of sale computer systems ensure speedy checkout in modern super-markets. *Courtesy of NCR Corp.*

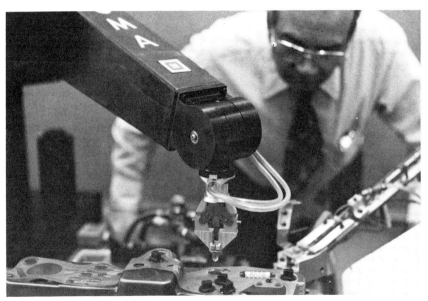

Figure 5.2 The programmable universal machine for assembly (PUMA) was developed to handle simple assembly of small, lightweight automotive components which account for about 90% of the parts in an automobile. *Courtesy of General Motors Corp.*

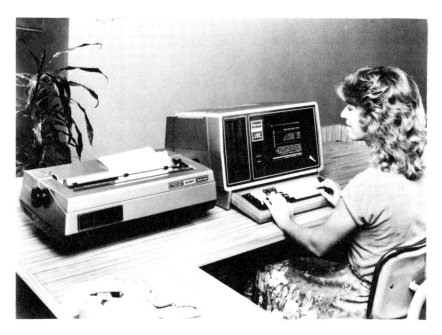

Figure 5.3   Computerized word processing makes the modern office more efficient.

Courtesy of Radio Shack, a division of Tandy Corp.

sell orders on that exchange. SIMPAC is a computerized simulation of trading strategies used in the training of floor brokers, stock specialists, and member firms. There is also QUOTRON, used by member firms to provide instant, up-to-the-minute stock price quotations.

2. Banking: Computers have been used for years by banking institutions to register transactions against customer accounts (Fig. 5.4). With the increasing volume of checks being processed (over 33 billion separate checks annually by 1980), we are rapidly approaching the limit to the number of checks that can be handled by our banks using current methods. The only reason so many can be handled now is that the MICR (magnetic ink character recognition) numbers on the bottom of virtually all American checks permit them to be processed by computer. We are seeing several new advances in the use of computers in banking:

*A. Automated tellers: These systems dispense money, receive deposits, and accept bill payments 24 hours a day from account holders with proper identification (Fig. 5.5). The automated tellers are often programmed to extend credit within predefined limits to account holders.

Figure 5.4   On-line systems connect the tellers terminal to a central computer allowing transactions to be handled electronically.   *Courtesy of NCR Corp.*

Figure 5.5   This automated teller in Jerusalem, Israel processes customer transactions 24 hours a day.   *Photo by Stephen R. Heller*

B. **Electronic funds transfer system (EFTS):** This trend toward further computerizaton of the banking function could replace cash and checks completely. All transfer of funds would be done through a computerized clearing house, perhaps in the form of a computer utility like the phone company, into which individual stores, employers and government would feed all financial transactions. Individuals would receive statements periodically or, upon demand, giving the status of their account. Both individuals and institutions would have to change the way they handle accounts, since there would no longer be a time lag in the transfer of money often called the **float.** Electronic transfer of funds would completely eliminate "playing the float" which now allows people to pay bills with money that hasn't been transferred yet!

Science
Computers have been used with great success in the scientific area to provide the answers to lengthy and very complicated computations.

1. Mathematical and statistical analysis: Although the theory for such analysis has been available in some cases for centuries, it was not until the development of general-purpose computing machines in the middle of the 20th century that the theory could be applied in any practical sense.

2. **Simulation:** Simulation is the technique of developing a dynamic computerized model of some real-life system using mathematical equations and variables. Probability theory is also used to introduce the element of chance. Simulations have given scientists many valuable insights about how systems will react to change. Simulations have been done for the U.S. economy, the human body, population trends and weather patterns. An example of a large simulation is an analysis of population, poverty, land and wealth distributions in a world-wide model.

3. Real-time experiments: Computers are used to monitor incoming data from actual experiments and to alter the value of certain parameters if necessary. For example, a computer could be receiving data from a radar station tracking a weather balloon and cause the course of the balloon to change based on programmed criteria (Fig. 5.6).

Health Care
Computers have become an indispensable tool in the delivery of good health care. They are used at every stage of health care: administrative, lab analysis, disease diagnosis, patient monitoring, control of artificial limbs, medical libraries, research, medical training. Just a few of these applications are described below.

Figure 5.6 A weather balloon containing automated tracking devices is launched.
Courtesy of NOAA.

*1. Administrative tasks: Computers are used by most hospitals to handle patient billing, insurance claims, room assignments and, in many cases, patients' diets and prescriptions.

2. Medical history files: Many medical centers and insurance companies are storing patient medical histories on computer. In Stockholm, Sweden, the entire population is on a medical data bank providing on-the-spot information in emergency situations. With such a system it is necessary to define and prevent unauthorized access to this very sensitive information.

3. Diagnosis: Computers are being used with increasing frequency to provide preliminary diagnosis of disease based on data from lab tests, which can be input directly into the computer (Fig. 5.7A and 5.7B).

*4 On-line patient monitoring: Computers are used to monitor vital signs and life-support systems during surgery and in intensive care units. They sound an alarm when any specified deviation occurs. They have also been used in catherizations into the heart chambers of heart attack victims, to monitor the most subtle activity of the heart.

5. Medical school: Patient simulations on computers help train medical students to recognize symptoms and to diagnose and treat disease. Students are able to use such a system to teach themselves, without serious consequence if the simulated "patient" dies.

Figure 5.7A   A medical technologist uses a blood analyzer which takes a drop of blood from a test tube, analyzes it with a laser beam and prints 8 results on a form in 60 seconds. This work formerly took two technicians one hour to accomplish.

Courtesy of Shady Grove Adventist Hospital, Rockville, MD.

Legal Profession and Law Enforcement

1. **Legal information retrieval systems:** Systems such as LEXIS (Fig. 5.8), the computerized law clerk, provide case citings, which are based on key words, faster and more thoroughly than a human could. For a citing of interest, the complete text of rulings or court cases can be requested.

*2. National Crime Information Center (NCIC): This is an automated police information network developed by the FBI in the 1960's and available to local police jurisdictions. Teletypes are installed at local police stations and connected by phone lines to state police centers. These centers are **on-line** to the computer at the FBI headquarters in Washington (Fig. 5.9). Immediate information is available on stolen cars, missing and wanted persons, lost and stolen property and securities, stolen guns, outstanding warrants, narcotic drug intelligence, suspended and revoked drivers' licenses, automobile registration, and arrest records.

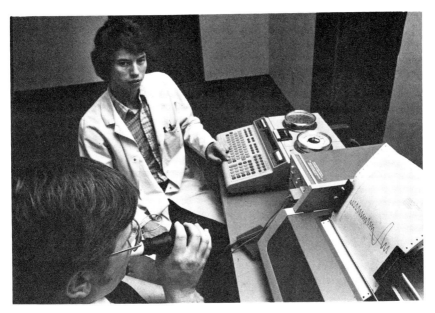

Figure 5.7B This Pulmonary Function System (HP-9825) Computer reports on a patient's physical state, by analyzing atmospheric pressure, temperature, and humidity and producing a printout of the breathing patterns.

Courtesy of Shady Grove Adventist Hospital, Rockville, MD.

3. Computerized court records and jury selection: This is an administrative application which has greatly aided the overloaded court systems (Fig. 5.10).

4. Security Systems: There are numerous sophisticated computer-controlled security systems. One of particular interest is the Midex 55 motion-sensing computer. It requires no sensors or special wiring. This system generates a harmless energy beam and sounds an alarm after the computer has interpreted the nature of any motion. The alarm shuts itself off if the intruder leaves.

Education

Computers have been used in education since the mid-1960's, beginning with administrative tasks such as personnel records and payrolls and evolving into student records maintenance and course scheduling. By the late 1960's and early 1970's, computers had found their way into the classroom.

*1. Guidance: Computerized guidance systems, such as the EXPLORE system developed in Maryland, are used to aid students in career and college selection. These systems can test the aptitudes, attitudes and work values of the student on the spot and provide information such as skill

Figure 5.8 LEXIS, the legal information retrieval system.

Courtesy of MEAD DATA Central.

Figure 5.9 The central computer system for the F.B.I National Crime Information Center (NCIC). *Courtesy of the F.B.I.*

THE WALL STREET JOURNAL
Thursday, May 28, 1981

Supreme Court Decides to Join Computer Age

By STEPHEN WERMEIL

Next October, for the first time since the Justices began issuing opinions in 1792, decisions will be printed by a computer. The changes are supported by Chief Justice Warren Burger, who recalls that when he arrived at the Supreme Court in 1969, "they didn't even have a Xerox machine in the building."

The idea to bring in computers originated with Mr. Burger in 1972. He says he wanted some statistics from the court clerk's office and discovered that office workers had to count cases from a handwritten log. "They were doing it the way they had done it in Civil War days," the Chief Justice says, "only they used ballpoints instead of quill pens."

The use of computers is also spreading to federal courts. Federal district and appeals courts have been experimenting, through the Federal Judicial Center in Washington, with a system called Courtran that would provide centralized management and docketing capability.

Figure 5.10   Excerpts from a Wall Street Journal article about computers used in the Supreme Court.
Reprinted by permission of Wall Street Journal, © Dow Jones & Co., Inc., 1981. All rights reserved.

level, experience needed, and job characteristics for many different occupations. They can provide similar information to aid in college selection.

 *2. **Computer Assisted Instruction (CAI):** The computer is used in classroom instruction to provide drill and practice exercises to reinforce concepts presented by the teacher (Fig. 5.11). The student receives immediate feedback about the correctness of the answer and can be given easier or harder exercises to work on based upon this feedback. The more advanced CAI systems, such as those used in high schools and colleges, are called tutorial systems because they present self-paced courses in which the computer introduces the concepts, provides the exercises, and does the testing. Students proceed at their own rate and see a teacher only for extra help. PLATO IV, developed originally by the Control Data Corporation at the University of Illinois, is an example of such a system. Through PLATO there are approximately 4,000 hours of instruction representing over 100 subject areas such as elementary mathematics and reading, secondary and college mathematics, physics, social sciences, foreign languages, medicine, law, veterinary medicine, nursing, music, physical education, and others. PLATO also has a feature called TUTOR which allows teachers to write their own lessons into the system.

3. **Computer Managed Instruction (CMI):** The computer is used to manage the instructional sequence for each child. Such a system is based on an educational model with clearly defined performance objectives. The children are tested against these performance objectives, and the teacher is provided with prescriptions for each child based on the testing. The process of retesting and represcribing continues until the performance objectives are met. Since each child is at a different level, there is the presumption of individualized instruction.

4. **LOGO** approach: This constitutes a radical departure from the passive role children play in the CAI and CMI applications. LOGO is a simple programming language designed to provide children with a problem-solving environment via computer programming. With LOGO children can write simple programs and manipulate a device called the LOGO turtle which generates the computer pictures called **graphics.** By using the computer as a tool for exploring mathematical and scientific concepts, children are learning how to think for themselves and to formulate problems on their own. Seymour Papert of MIT described the value of teaching children how to program in his 1969 article "Teaching Children Thinking" and in his recent book *Mindstorms*.

Figure 5.11   Computer assisted instruction (CAI) teaches children to use a computer.

Photo by Dave Martin.

Library Science

Computers have radically affected the maintenance of information. Access to materials in a library is frequently handled by computer filing systems and also by computer check-out of books (Fig. 5.12). The Library of Congress maintains a sophisticated computerized search system based on titles, authors and key words.

Figure 5.12   Computerized checkout of library books.   *Photo by Dave Martin.*

Clarkson College in Potsdam, New York opened an educational resource center in 1981. This center is designed to be much more than a college library. The center has 60 terminals from which students can do on-line searches of the books and microfiche in the library's collection. In addition, students have access to over 150 national data bases in order to search for information. One such data base, ERIC (Educational Resources Information Center), is a federally funded, nationwide system designed to collect information about current developments in education and make it available to the public. Much of the research for this book, *Bits 'n Bytes About Computing,* was the result of an ERIC search.

Space Applications

Due to the technical nature of many of these applications, they are simply listed below:

1. Tracking space vehicles.
2. Mission control.

3. Missile guidance.
4. Navigation.
5. Monitoring astronauts' body functions during space experiments and exploration.
6. Simulations research analysis.

Transportation

*1. Traffic control: In most large cities there are computer-controlled traffic switching systems which can be used to control the flow of traffic by adjusting the red-green light cycles. Much of the California freeway system is monitored by computer.

*2. Air traffic control: Radar data is put directly into computerized monitors to help the human flight controllers direct traffic (Fig. 5.13). All commercial pilot training is now done on computer simulators, which provide experience with numerous situations that a pilot might encounter while flying the airplane.

3. Train and subway switching systems: The BART system (Bay Area Rapid Transit) in San Francisco and the METRO system in Washington, D.C., are two examples of sophisticated, real-time computer systems used to control the scheduling of trains, subways, and buses (Fig. 5.14).

4. Freight handling: The allocation of freight on trucks, buses, and planes is done to a great extent by computer. It is particularly important that each load be maximized to conserve energy by eliminating unnecessary trips.

*5. Automobile maintenance: Systems such as the computerized engine diagnosis developed by Volkswagen and the Exhaust Performance Analyzer used in Chicago to test exhaust fumes are examples of how the computer is being used in maintaining automobiles.

Communications and Information Dissemination

Perhaps one of the ways in which computers will most dramatically change our lives will be the way we receive information in the future. Below are some computer information systems already in operation.

1. Communication **networks**: Orbiting communication satellites whose path and signals are computer-controlled have already made world-wide radio and TV broadcasting possible as well as telephone access to most of the world (Fig. 5.15). Telephone technology both for long lines and local areas is highly competitive and is changing rapidly due to microcomputer circuitry and microwave transmission.

Figure 5.13 View of the computer area of the Automated Radar Tracking System (TRACON) and a tower cab with a BRITE scope remotely connected to TRACON.

Courtesy of FAA and PATCO.

Figure 5.14 In Washington D.C. the METRO trains are dispatched by an operator using a computerized system. *WMATA photo by Paul Myatt.*

2. Electronic newspapers: Columbus, Ohio launched the nation's first commercial electronic newspaper, CompuServe, on July 1, 1980. Subscribers with a home computer terminal can call up the contents of the Columbus Dispatch daily. Other metropolitan dailies are joining the service, providing users access to the top newspapers across the nation.

3. Computerized information systems: A remarkable information system called VIEW DATA has been developed by the British Post Office. The three components of the system arc the consumer with a specially modified TV set, the computer and telephone lines for data transmission, and the information suppliers who provide the actual text. Already available throughout Great Britain, the system is now being linked to Holland, Germany, and Canada and is also being made compatible with a similar French system. VIEW DATA provides newspapers, magazines, local activites (i.e., theater, movie, restaurant listings), traffic bulletins, stock market reports, sports scores and standings, airline and hotel fare and reservation service, and the list goes on.

   In the United States an information utility called the SOURCE is being marketed with features similar to VIEW DATA (Fig. 5.16). The SOURCE operates from a home terminal, a screen and a telephone coupler. A printer is an optional feature providing a hard copy of anything desired. The Encyclopedia Brittannica is now available on the SOURCE. It is not hard to envision entire libraries available in our homes at our fingertips in the future!

*4. Opinion Polls: There are on-line, computer-based opinion polls, which allow viewer feedback, available in several major cities in the United States. The QUBE system, in Columbus, Ohio, allows a television viewer to respond to opinion questions. The question appears on the TV screen. The viewer then presses a button on a special device installed in the home and a central computer immediately tabulates the responses. The results of the tabulation appear on the TV screen.

Government

Computers are used by local, state, and federal government agencies. Just a few of the uses are described below:

*1. Record keeping: Most government files are now maintained on computer. This includes everything from dog licensing, motor vehicle registration, tax records, and welfare and health care records and payments at the local level, to civil service employment, military personnel, Internal Revenue Service, Veteran's Administration, and Social Security Administration records at the federal level (Fig. 5.17).

Figure 5.15 Control center for a satellite network.   *Courtesy of COMSAT.*

2. City Planning: Computers are used to predict population patterns and to project urban development. These affect zoning regulations and support services such as fire, police, sanitation and education.

*3. **Computer-assisted dispatch systems (CADS):** These systems are used throughout the country to send fire, paramedic, and police personnel and equipment to the scenes of accidents and disasters (Fig. 5.18). Many of these systems not only simplify the dispatch process, but have sophisticated graphics capabilities which produce multicolored street maps, locations of fire hydrants, locations of other rescue units, and even the details of building layouts, special equipment and hazardous materials of major buildings in a city.

4. Military: Computers have a wide variety of uses in the military services including maintenance of personnel records, allocation of manpower, design and control of weapons, early warning and attack systems, tactical simulations (war games), and intelligence data gathering and storing. It is interesting to note that MARK I, the first general-purpose digital computer developed in 1944, was designed to meet a military need: the production of ballistic weapons tables for the new weapons developed during World War II.

```
>data liball

               *** THE SOURCE ***

ADVANCED APPLICATIONS & PROGRAMS.................DATA ADAPPR
AIRSCHEDULES....................................DATA AIRSCHED
ANNOUNCEMENTS (UPDATED FREQUENTLY)...............DATA ANNOUN
ASTROLOGY LIBRARY ..............................DATA ASTRO-LIB
AWARE FINANCIAL SERVICE.........................DATA AFS
BRIDGE ACCORDING TO THROOP......................DATA BRIDGE
BUSINESS & FINANCE..............................DATA BIZDEX
CLASSIFIED ADS & BULLETIN BOARD.................DATA CLASSI
CONSUMER INFORMATION............................DATA CONSUM
CROSS X-ASSEMBLERS..............................INFO X-ASSEMBLERS
DINING OUT:  WASHINGTON, D.C....................RESTGD
             NEW YORK CITY......................NYRESTGD
DISCOUNT SHOPPING SERVICE (MONEY SAVERS).........DATA BUCKS
EDUCATION.......................................DATA EDUCAT
ENERGY SAVING NEWS & TIPS.......................ENERGY
FINANCIAL NEWS..................................DATA BIZDEX
GAMES...........................................DATA GAMES
HOME ENTERTAINMENT..............................DATA HOMENT
INFORMATION ON DEMAND...........................DATA IOD
MAILCALL........................................DATA MAILCALL
MAIL DELIVERY...................................INFO DATAPOST
NEW YORK TIMES NEWS SUMMARY.....................DATA NYTNS

NEW YORK TIMES CONSUMER DATA BASE...............NYTCDB
PERSONAL CALENDAR & NOTEBOOK....................DATA PERSON
PERSONAL FINANCE................................DATA PERSFI
POLITICAL ACTION REPORT.........................DATA PAR
RAYLUX FINANACIAL SERVICES......................DATA FINANCIAL
SCIENCE & ENGINEERING...........................DATA SCIENG
SELF-PERCEPTION.................................DATA ESP, DATA LORE
SPORTS..........................................DATA SPORTS
SUGGESTION BOX..................................DATA SUGBOX
TRAVEL CLUB.....................................DATA TRAVEL
UNITED PRESS INTERNATIONAL (UPI)................DATA DANEWS
USER DIRECTORY..................................DATA USEDIR
VOICEGRAM.......................................DATA VOICEGRAM
WEATHER.........................................DATA WEATHR
WISDOM OF THE AGES..............................WISDOM
```

Figure 5.16   Menu of information offered by the SOURCE.

Courtesy of the SOURCE Telecomputing Corp.

5. House Information System (HIS): A computer system in the U.S. House of Representatives provides instant information on the status of any bill introduced, a daily legislative calendar, computerized constituent mailing lists for each House member, and an automated roll call vote at stations positioned around the floor of the House. A similar system, called LEGIS, is used by the U.S. Senate (Fig. 5.19).

*6. **Letter Mail Code Sorting Service (LMCSS):** The U.S. Postal Service is using a computer system for automated letter sorting.

United States Department of State
Bureau of Consular Affairs
Passport Services

Your new Machine Readable Passport (MRP) is an historic document - the world's first passport with machine readable capability

Your new Machine Readable Passport is an historic U.S. Government document. It is one of the first passports to be issued under automated systems technology, and marks a major breakthrough by the Department of State in more efficient and economical service to the United States' international traveling public.

The Personal Data page located on the inside cover of your passport is divided into two parts - the upper section for *visual* purposes, the lower lines (white section) for machine readable purposes. This format accords with standards of automated passport control at major ports of entry around the world set by the International Civil Aviation Organization. The reflective laminated cover protects the machine readable and visual data on the page.

International standards will provide greater ease in the handling of your passport by customs, immigration and health officials. In the future they will also aid with automated processes in international airline reservations, preparation of manifest lists and financial transactions.

The Machine Readable Passport is expected to become available at all Passport Agencies in the United States by the end of 1985. It is a very valuable personal document issued by the United States Government - guard it carefully.

Norbert J. Krieg
Deputy Assistant Secretary
for Passport Services

Figure 5.17 A technician from the Passport Office enters data into the new computerized passport system. *Courtesy of the Bureau of Consular Affairs.*

Figure 5.18 A fireman monitors the computer-assisted dispatch system (CADS) in Montgomery County, Maryland. *Photo by Daniel Reich.*

Figure 5.19 Legislative assistant to Sen. Murkoski of Alaska uses the LEGIS terminal to obtain information about pending legislation in the Senate.   *Photo by Dave Martin.*

7. Census data gathering and analysis: As noted in the section about the history of computing, without modern computational devices, the enormous job of gathering and tabulating the census would have been impossible by the year 1890!

Politics

*1. Computerized campaigning: Computers are used to produce "personal" letters to constituents, to organize phone calling lists, and to compile results of opinion polls on the issues.

2. TV vote projections: Using past voting patterns and sophisticated statistical analysis techniques, a computer program can predict quite accurately the outcome of elections with only a small sample of data, such as the early returns. This is an area of public concern because it is felt by some that projections from one part of the country will influence the vote in another part. In fact, news media in Canada are not allowed to project winners in a locality until all the polling places are closed.

Leisure

1. Professional sports: Computers are used to provide information on player statistics (batting averages, yardages gained, etc.), player drafts,

and game play analysis. Professional sports have become as technological as they are commercial.

2. Computerized score keeping: The score-boards seen at the Olympics are computer controlled. Much of the timing and distance measurements are also done by computer.

*3. Computer games: There is a wide range of computer-based games available for all ages - Simon or Touch Me for children, and Star-Trek, Chess, Go, and Dungeons and Dragons for the adult computer hobbyist. The Sesame Street theme park in Philadelphia has a room full of computer games as one of its main attractions (Fig. 5.20). Games such as Lemonade Stand and Guess the Muppet allow children of all ages to pit themselves against the computer.

4. Computer produced art, music, poetry and dance: There is growing interest in using the computer as a creative medium. It has amazing capabilities to produce an infinite variety of patterns and colors. There have been some outstanding computer-produced cartoons and movies. There was even a set of computer-generated ''paintings'' similar in style to those of the painter Mondrian. Interestingly enough, the computer-produced art was judged by some to be more pleasing than the original artist's work.

Figure 5.20 Seventy computer consoles in the computer gallery at the family play park, Sesame Place in Pennsylvania, provide dozens of games for ages 3 and up.

Courtesy of Sesame Place.

Much has been done in the field of music with computers. There are specially designed programming languages which enable musicians to orchestrate entire musical works and in some cases to translate that into actual sound waves (Fig. 5.21).

Figure 5.21   A music synthesizer hooked to a microcomputer which can be used to compose and experiment with music.   *Photo by Paul Hoffman.*

At least one poet is using the computer to write his poetry by experimenting with color and words. He uses different colors for different poetical constructions and mood words to produce stronger feelings with his poetry than the simple printed page. For example, the word "happy" might appear in yellow letters and in the alliteration "bouncing baby boy" each letter "b" would be highlighted in the same color.

Dancers, too, can use computers. Special computer languages have been designed so that a choreographer can enter dance movements into the computer. These dance routines are displayed on the video screen. The choreographer can view the dance from many angles before teaching the routine to dancers (Fig. 5.22).

KEY IDEAS

User
Real-Time Applications
GIGO
Point of sale marketing

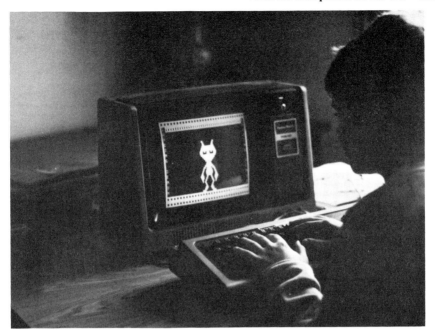

Figure 5.22   The program Dancing Demon allows the user to choreograph dances and create accompanying melodies.   *Photo by Dave Martin.*

Management Information Systems (MIS)
Word Processing
Electronic Funds Transfer System (EFTS)
Simulation
Information Storage and Retrieval
Computer Assisted Instruction (CAI)
Computer Managed Instruction (CMI)
LOGO
Data Base
Network
Computer Assisted Dispatch System (CADS)
Letter Mail Code Sorting Service (LMCSS)

ACTIVITIES

See For Yourself
      Arrange for a visit to one of the following places where computers are being used:
      local business
      fire station
      library

grocery store
local government office

Here are some things to find out about:

1. What major things does the computer do for them?
2. How long have they used computers?
3. How was the job accomplished before the computer came?
4. What types of information are stored, processed, and created by the computer?
5. How is the information put into the computer?
6. How is the information put out by the computer?
7. Who are the people who use and operate the computer?
8. Are the people who use the computer system pleased with it?

TEACHER'S CORNER
Purpose: To provide the experience of seeing and finding out about a computer application in a setting relevant to the student's background.
Materials: Teacher created worksheet.
Time: 1/2-day trip.
Skills: Communication, observation, writing.
Additional Information: The teacher can arrange a trip for the entire class or have the students arrange their own visits by sending business letters or making business phone calls. The teacher should encourage students to ask the interviewee questions when they go for their visit.

What's My Line?
    Based on the information you have gathered in your visit, form a panel of students to play the roles of businessman, computer manufacturer, government official, and any others you have found. Discuss how computers are used in their fields.

TEACHER'S CORNER
Purpose: To reinforce the ideas learned when observing a computer facility by verbalizing these ideas.
Materials: Tables, chairs set up for a panel discussion.
Time: Assignment for one or two weeks.
Skills: Verbal, written, research, organization.

Pen Pals
    Write a business letter to a computer company asking for information about their computer hardware or software.

TEACHER'S CORNER
Purpose: To practice the skill of writing business letters in a computer applications context.
Materials: Paper, pencil, pen.
Time: 15-30 minutes.
Skills: Written expressions, neatness.
Additional Information: A good source of addresses is the professional computing magazines.

Poster Talks

Prepare an oral report and a poster about the use of computers in some area of life such as medicine, government, education, transportation, or sports.

TEACHER'S CORNER
Purpose: To provide a vehicle for researching current literature on a timely subject.
Materials: Current magazines and books about computers, poster paper or construction paper, markers.
Time: One to two week project at home.
Skills: Research, written and verbal expression, art.

Lawful Learning

Invite a police officer to your classroom to tell how computers are used in law enforcement.

TEACHER'S CORNER
Purpose: To learn about how computers are used in law enforcement.
Materials: Guest police officer.
Time: 45 minutes to an hour.
Skills: Listening, observing.

Computer Olympics

Have the students bring in any computer games they have and arrange a games rally. Afterwards, think how these games were programmed. Which ones did you like best?

TEACHER'S CORNER
Purpose: To stimulate thinking about how the electronic games work.
Materials: Electronic games brought in by students.
Time: One hour.
Skills: Memory, logical thinking, verbal expression, manual dexterity.
Additional Information: The teacher could incorporate this lesson into a consu-

mer awareness lesson. Have the students research the cost and battery needs of the games and make a comparison chart of the games' pros and cons.

Business Cents

Pretend you are starting a business to sell and repair bicycles. Make a list of files that you would need to run your business such as an employees file, a customer file, a parts file. List all the information that you would want to keep in each file.

TEACHER'S CORNER

Purpose: To reinforce the concept of data files, what they are, and why the are needed by businesses.
Materials: Paper, pencils.
Time: 30-45 minutes.
Skills: Reasoning, written expression.

That's Life

Arrange for the class to play a simulation game such as the *Game of Life* (Scientific American, October 1970).

TEACHER'S CORNER

Purpose: To illustrate how a simulation works.
Materials: One or more simulation type games which show some real process taking place through the playing of a game.
Time: 1-2 hours depending upon the game.
Skills: Reasoning, memory, following rules.
Additional Information: Many good simulation games exist for the election process or the westward movement. These could be incorporated into your social studies unit. If you have a computer, look into the simulation games available on your computer.

Information Please

If you live near a computerized information service, arrange for a visit to see how it works.

TEACHER'S CORNER

Purpose: To familiarize students with electronic information services such as the SOURCE or ERIC.
Materials: Access to a computerized information service.
Time: One hour to 1/2-day trip.
Skills: Reading, observing.
Additional Information: Many university libraries and public libraries have these services available.

Pretty As A Picture

When a picture is sent from outer space, it is sent as a series of digits. These digits are then decoded to represent varying shades of darkness and light. Based on the sequence of digits, the picture is formed in a grid. For example, if 0 means no color and 1 means black, the series of digits 010,010,111 would form a picture in a three by three grid.

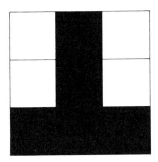

Use a five by five grid to show the picture formed by the series of digits 10100,10101,11100,10101,10101. Remember 0 means no color and 1 means black.

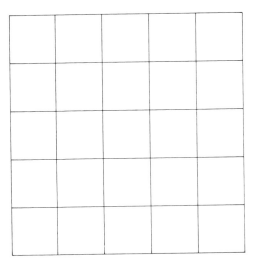

TEACHER'S CORNER

Purpose: To provide an introduction to computer graphics.

Materials: A teacher created worksheet.

Time: 15 minutes.

Skills: Sequencing, following instructions.

Additional Information: The students should be encouraged to form their own pictures using the digitized picture technique.

Articles Galore

Get out the articles you have been collecting. Arrange them in appropriate categories such as computers in science, computers in art, computers and the handicapped. Mount them so they can be displayed on the bulletin board.

TEACHER'S CORNER

Purpose: To foster an awareness of the many areas in which computers are being used.
Materials: Articles collected (see "Watch Dog" activity in Chapter 2), poster board, glue, scissors.
Time: Ongoing project.
Skill: Classification.
Additional Information: Some of the stories might be about the same news item written from different points of view. This activity could be incorporated into a study of newspapers. The students should note differing story "angles" on the same subject.

Students can form a histogram from the articles. The class should note in which areas computer impact is being discussed most in the popular media.

Scavenger Hunt

Make a collection of items that use computers, are products of computers, or are associated with computers. Here's a list to get you started. Add things from your everyday life to the list.

...computer printed grocery tape...picture of computer games in an arcade...ad for home computer...ad for digital watch...library card using a computer...receipt from automated teller...computer printed report...album cover or ad for computer generated music...universal product code...

TEACHER'S CORNER

Purpose: This activity is designed to help students become more aware of the many ways that computers are used in daily life.
Materials: Teacher created worksheet.
Time: One week or ongoing project.
Skills: Reading, verbalization.
Additional Information: The items collected could be used to make a bulletin board display or sharing center in the classroom.

RELATED READINGS

(**S** -Student, **T** -Teacher)
1. Berger, Melvin. *Computers in Your Life.* Thomas Crowell, 1981. (**S,T**)
2. Brown, John. *Computers and Automation.* ARCO Publishing Company, 1968. (**S,T**)

3. Dorf, Richard. *Computers and Man*. Second Edition, Boyd and Fraser Publishing Company, 1977. (**T**)

4. Graham, Neill. *The Mind Tool: Computers and Their Impact on Society*. West Publishing Company, 1980. (**S,T**)

5. Halas, John (editor). *Computer Animation*. Visual Communications Book, 1975. (**T**)

6. Hawkes, Nigel. *The Computer Revolution*. E.P.Dutton, 1971. (**S,T**)

7. Holorein, Martin. *Computers and Their Societal Impact*. John Wiley and Sons, 1977. (**S,T**)

8. Leavitt, Ruth (editor). *Artist and Computers*. Creative Computing Press, 1976. (**T**)

9. Logsdon, Tom. *Computers and Social Controversy*. Computer Science Press, 1980. (**T**)

10. McCauley, Carole. *Computers and Creativity*. Praeger Publishers, 1975. (**T**)

11. Morgan, Christopher. *The Byte Book of Computer Music*. Byte Books. (**T**)

12. Papert, Seymour. *Mindstorms*. Basic Books, 1980. (**T**)

13. Sanders, Donald. *Computers and Society*. McGraw-Hill, 1973. (**T**)

14. Silver, Gerald. *The Social Impact of Computers*. Harcourt Brace Jovanovich, 1979. (**T**)

15. Smith, Robert. *Privacy, How to Protect What's Left of It*. Doubleday & Company, Anchor Press, 1979. (**T**)

16. Spencer, Donald. *Computers in Society: Wheres, Whys and Hows of Computer Use*. Hayden Book Company, 1975. (**T**)

17. Waite, Mitchell. *Computer Graphics Primer*. Howard W. Sams and Company, 1979. (**T**)

Chapter 6

Where Do We Fit into the Computer Picture?

CAREERS IN COMPUTING

The computer field is a rapidly changing and expanding one with career opportunities at all levels. There is hardly a business or profession which does not use computers in some way. The purpose of this unit is to explore the opportunities available now and to predict the near future. We will examine the personal characteristics of a computer professional as well as the level of skill and training required for the different jobs. Our educational objective is to provide enough career information to enable the students to begin to realistically assess their own interests and potential in the field (1). This chapter is written to enable the teacher to provide career guidance to the student.

Personal Traits of a Computer Professional
One exciting feature of the computer field is the remarkable variety of careers (Fig. 6.1). There are many different ways to be involved:

Design, build, or maintain computer equipment.
Design programs that instruct computers how to solve problems.
Undertake research and development.
Work in business, in academia, or in government.
Work independently or as part of a team.
Take interesting jobs almost anywhere in the world.

What personal characteristics and skills are needed? A keen interest in and curiosity about computers and their applications are a sure sign that one should pursue this field. As in many vocations, good oral and written communication skills, a sense of responsibility, and an ability to reason logically are needed. Many professional positions require specialized knowledge of mathematics or engineering as well as knowledge of computer equipment and applications programs.

Figure 6.1   There are numerous careers in computing at all levels of training.

EDUCATION AND TRAINING

Career opportunities depend strongly on education and training. The first step is to carefully evaluate talents and interests and then to choose an educational goal from vocational training, data processing schools, colleges, universities, and graduate school.

The next step is to consider taking a data processing aptitude test. A sample of such a test is included in Figure 6.2. Another possibility is to take a beginning programming course. This provides the added benefit of an introduction to computers.

INSTRUCTIONS FOR PART I

In Part I you will be given some problems like those on this page. The letters in each series follow a certain rule. For each series of letters you are to find the correct rule and complete the series. One of the letters on the right side of the paper is the correct answer.

INSTRUCTIONS FOR PART II

In Part II each row is a problem. Each row consists of four figures on the left-hand side of the page and five figures on the right-hand side of the page. The four figures on the left make a series. You are to find out which one of the figures on the right-hand side would be the next or the fifth one in the series.

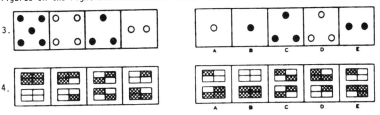

Figure 6.2   Typical questions from a programmer aptitude test.

Courtesy of Computer Learning Center of Washington, D.C.

Vocational programs are usually available after the tenth grade. School counselors are trained to determine which students are eligible. Vocational school graduates are trained for important roles, such as a **data entry clerk** who types information into the computer system, a **computer operator** who oversees the running of the equipment, or a **maintenance engineer** who keeps the computer in working order.

Data processing schools usually concentrate on computer maintenance, operator training, and programming (Fig. 6.3). However, additional education may be required to be eligible for advancement or promotion. Not all coursework is transferable with credit to colleges or universities. Before enrolling, students should investigate academic programs and consult with people in computer related jobs.

Community colleges usually offer one and two year programs to train data entry clerks and computer operators (Fig. 6.4). They also offer two-year programs that may qualify the student to be a beginning programmer. The credit in such a program is often transferable to a bachelor's degree program. A community college education may enable the student to obtain a job with an employer willing to pay for additional education.

Colleges and universities offer bachelor's degree programs which provide entry into many computer related positions including **programmer, computer architect, systems programmer,** and **systems analyst.** They also provide in-

Figure 6.3 A Tape Librarian catalogues and locates computer tapes at the FBI Computer Center Tape Library.   *Courtesy of the F.B.I.*

Figure 6.4 A computer operator at the National Crime Information Center consults with a shift supervisor.   *Courtesy of the F.B.I.*

terdisciplinary curricula so that computing interests can be combined with studies in other fields.

Remember: Students interested in a computing career should begin preparing for it NOW by taking all the mathematics they can!

CASE STUDIES

Computing has many specialties. Engineers design new computers matched with each new level of technology. Applications programmers write programs for specific tasks in business, government, science, or engineering. Systems programmers write programs that run computers themselves or serve as tools for other programmers. Where do you fit in? Perhaps your own interests and talents appear in one of the following examples.

Betty became interested in computers when she had a programming course in high school. She went to a state university where she majored in computer science. She is now a **systems programmer.**

"Systems programmers write programs to help others communicate with a computer. I worked on a project to write a compiler for a new computer. This compiler translates programs written in the FORTRAN programming language into the machine language of the new computer. In a few years I plan to form a company which will specialize in writing compilers."

On Monday evenings Betty participates in a program sponsored by the local chapter of her computer society and a United Way agency, which **teaches computing** to high school students.

"I had the greatest thrill the other day. John, a blind student I have been working with, told me that he has decided to take more math next semester. He is collecting catalogues of colleges that have computer science programs. John is bright and should do well in computing. There are braille and audio terminals which can make him less dependent on the sighted reader. Computing is an especially good field for the disabled."

Robert got his degree in business administration, with concentration on information processing. His first job was as an **applications programmer** for a manufacturing company. His projects varied from controlling the inventory in the company's local warehouse to calculating tax deductions on payroll checks. After two years the company offered him a promotion to **systems analyst.**

"I became a systems analyst because I enjoy working with people. A manager comes and describes a problem to me. I investigate to see if the computer can help solve the problem. If it can, we work together to develop a precise statement of the problem and a clear definition of the desired results. I then work with a programmer to write the programs that meet the specifications. It's very satisfying to oversee a problem from the planning stage to the final answer."

Mary is an electrical engineer working as a **computer architect.** After graduation, she joined an aircraft company working on the space shuttle for the National Aeronautics and Space Administration (NASA). She helped design an on-board computer and wrote programs for it. Now she writes programs that simulate the behavior of the space shuttle; these programs will be used to train pilots.

"Life is never dull around here. Yesterday I worked with equations; today I work with the astronauts; tomorrow I'll write a training manual. Which reminds me, I always knew math was important, but no one ever told me how important writing skills are. My advice is to take all the math AND English you can."

Jose manages a commercial computer center. Many small companies use this center rather than buy a computer of their own. Some of the companies have their own programmers, some use Jose's staff.

"I studied data processing at a community college. My first job was as a **computer operator.** I soon found that helping people use the computer was more interesting than operating one—so I decided to return to school for a degree in information systems. Luckily, part-time jobs are plentiful. I was able to work as an operator at night and go to school during the day."

After graduation Jose worked as an **applications programmer.** He was promoted to **senior programmer** and later to manager of a group of programmers.

"As a manager I work with a lot of people and budgets, but I rely heavily on my knowledge of computers during technical reviews of my staff. Now I am back in school working on a master's degree in business administration at night—but this time my company is paying."

William has been in computing for twenty years. "When I got my degree there weren't any computer science departments. I majored in mathematics and took the two computer courses offered at the university. Now the department is called Mathematics and Computer Sciences." William worked as a **scientific programmer** for an oil company. "My first programming assignment was with the geophysics group, developing a program for interpreting seismic data. Several years later I decided I was ready for a graduate degree. I got one of the first Ph.D. degrees in computer science and became a **professor.** I really enjoy working with students, conducting research in new aspects of computing—and still there is time to help others as a **consultant.** (Fig. 6.5).

"Most of my clients are government agencies in the less developed countries. I advise them in various ways, from how to use computers in the petroleum industry to how to process census data. Last year I was in the Middle East and Africa. Next summer I will be working with the United Nations to ad vise a Latin American country on computer science education."

Figure 6.5   An instructor uses a microcomputer to teach a student.

Courtesy of Apple Computer Inc.

Job Potential

This industry is dynamic and growing. Career opportunities abound. Individuals can enter the computer field directly from high school as computer operators or data entry clerks. They can receive on-the-job training while attending college. They can be programmers, then systems analysts, and ultimately **software project managers.** They can even start their own software company or computer store.

Training is available in computer maintenance and repair in the military. With a background in electrical engineering one can design computing equipment, then become a chief engineer and ultimately a project manager.

Although there are numerous paths in computing, many computer people obtain a bachelor's degree in a technical field such as computer science, electrical engineering or information systems before entering the job market. Some continue to graduate school.

Computer technology is everywhere, from lifesaving intensive care units to pleasurable toys. Computer technology has been of special help to handicapped people, many of whom have become productive computer professionals.

There are many sources of information about jobs, salaries, specialties, and other aspects of computer careers. The school counselor may be able to provide such information. So may libraries and state agencies. The U.S.

Department of Labor publishes the Occupational Outlook Handbook and the Dictionary of Occupational Titles, which are available in the school library, public library, or through the Bureau of Labor Statistics, 441 G Street, N.W., Washington D.C. 20212.

KEY IDEAS

Data Entry Clerk
Programmer
  Applications Programmer
  Systems Programmer
  Scientific Programmer
Systems Analyst
Computer Operator
Computer Maintenance Engineer
Computer Architect
Consultant
Software Project Manager

ACTIVITIES

Business Sense
Identify and learn about companies and other organizations in your area that have computer installations.

TEACHER'S CORNER
Purpose: To help the students learn about career opportunities in the computer field.
Time: One week.
Skills: Verbal expression, research.
Additional Information: The teacher may want to assign teams of students to do the activities in this section and report back to the class.

See For Yourself
Arrange to go to:
1. A Company or organization that uses computers, to see the computers there.
2. A local computer store to see a demonstation of the computers sold there.

TEACHER'S CORNER
Purpose: To help students learn about career opportunities in the computer field.
Time: One week.
Skills: Verbal expression, observation.

Write On!
Write to computer manufacturers and request information about their products, services and career opportunities.

TEACHER'S CORNER

Purpose: To help students learn about career opportunities in the computer field as well as to practice writing business letters.
Materials: Pen, paper, addresses of computer firms.
Time: 30 minutes.
Skills: Written expression, neatness.
Additional Information: Try the yellow pages or computing magazines for addresses of computer manufacturers. Look to your local community first.

Wanted!
Read the want ads in your local newspaper and in computer publications to see what jobs are being offered and what qualifications are being sought. Post some of these ads on your classroom bulletin board.

TEACHER'S CORNER

Purpose: To help the student learn about careers in computers as well as to learn how to use classified ads.
Materials: Local newspapers, computer magazines.
Time: One or two weeks.
Skills: Reading comprehension, research.
Follow-Up: The teacher may also want to have the students write mock resumes or letters responding to the want ads to give them the experience of replying to a want ad and asking for a job.

On the Job
Arrange to listen:
1. To someone speak about careers in computing. Your teacher will arrange for a parent or computer professional to come in to speak to the class.
2. To a panel discusssion which includes someone who has been in the computer field for 20 years or so, someone new in the field, and someone who uses computers in his or her job, but is not a computer expert.

TEACHER'S CORNER

Purpose: To help students learn about career opportunities in the computing field.
Time: One hour.
Skills: Listening, comprehension, verbal expression.

Plan Ahead

Contact your local state employment agency to learn about job opportunities and to obtain additional career planning information.

TEACHER'S CORNER

Purpose: To help students learn about career opportunities in the computing field.

Time: One week.

Skills: Verbal expression, written expression, reading comprehension.

Additional Information: The teacher may choose to use a nearby college career placement office or high school career counseling facility if there is not a government employment office near. Similarly, a private employment agency may also be willing to provide information to the students.

RELATED READINGS

(**S** -Student, **T** -Teacher)

1. Baker, Eugene. *I Want to be a Computer Operator.* Children's Press, 1973. (**S**)
2. Edwards, Judith. *Elements of Computer Careers.* Prentice-Hall, Inc., 1977. (**S,T**)
3. Goldreich, Gloria, Goldreich, Esther. *What Can She Be? A Computer Scientist.* Lothrop, Lee and Shephard Co., 1979. (**S,T**)
4. Korotkin, Arthur. *A Study of the Use of Computers in The Development of Science Career Awareness in Elementary School Children.* Gibboney Associates, Inc., Kensington, Md. 20752. (**T**)
5. Lewis, Brenda. *"Careers in Computing."* New Univ, Vol. 3, No. 7, November 1969. (**T**)
6. Ray, JoAnne. *Careers in Computers.* Lerner Publications Co., 1975. (**S,T**)
7. Speedie, Stuart M. *Elements of Computer Careers.* AEDS Monitor, November 1973. (**T**)

ACKNOWLEDGEMENT

Many thanks to Dr. Richard Austing of the University of Maryland and others who authored "A Look into Computer Careers" for AFIPS (American Federation of Information Processing Societies) and granted permission to use that booklet in this chapter.

Chapter 7

How Will Computers Affect Our Lives?

THE SOCIAL IMPACT OF COMPUTERS

The objectives of this chapter are subjective by necessity. How deeply you can cover the topics depends upon the age and the maturity of your students. However, the issues are so important that every student should have exposure to them.

Many excellent books and articles have been written on the subject of computers and society, some of which are referenced in the bibliography. This section will provide only an overview to whet your appetite for further reading. The philosophy of this book is that computers are not inherently evil, but can be misused to produce results which are not in the interest of society. Any attempt to categorize use or misuse of computers is risky, because there is much disagreement as to what is or is not in the best interest of society.

PROTECTING INDIVIDUAL RIGHTS

Privacy

The **privacy** issue has probably generated more publicity during the last 15 years than any other issue. Former Supreme Court Justice Brandeis described the concept of privacy as the "right to be let alone —the most comprehensive of rights and the right most valued by civilized men." Former Justice Douglas characterized privacy as the freedom of the individual "to select for himself the time and circumstances when he will share his secrets with others and to what extent." Privacy thus defined is infringed upon by the collection of details about a person's private life, no matter how accurately or carefully it is done. Even more offensive is the dissemination of that information to others, whether they be private or public users of that information (Fig. 7.1).

Figure 7.1   How will we protect our privacy?

It must be noted, however, that to keep a complex, prosperous society operating efficiently, three resources are needed: energy, materials, and information. For example, accurate information about weather conditions, seed response, harvest time, etc., over a decade, helped to produce new varieties of rice and wheat which have tripled per-acre food production in India. More personal information, such as medical histories, has helped produce findings about cancer-causing agents in our food and environment. Population distribution information based on the census helps with the distribution of federal funds to local jurisdictions. To be responsible citizens in this computer age, we will have to be informed enough to make difficult decisions balancing society's needs for information against our own right to privacy.

The proliferation of computerized data files and large data banks containing personal information about individuals is viewed by many people as a threat to our privacy at the very least. Even more serious, they see the collection of such data as an assault on our civil liberties. Such concerns have not been entirely unwarranted. In the past there have been documented abuses by credit bureaus using regional credit files, by insurance companies using medical histories, and by law enforcement personnel using the FBI's National Crime Information Center (NCIC) arrest and surveillance records.

Attempts to consolidate all federal files into a national data bank have been staunchly resisted thus far. The resulting concern over files containing information about individuals has produced the Freedom of Information Act of 1966-67, the Fair Credit Reporting Act of 1970, and the Privacy Act of 1974. Many people feel that even stronger legislation is needed to insure our rights in this computerized age.

Depersonalization

A related concern is the **depersonalization** caused when people become numbers in a data file. Although Isaac Asimov, famous science fiction writer, suggests that a number is actually far more personal than a name - completely unique, more precise, and more apt to be correctly filed and manipulated - most people still feel dehumanized when they are referred to by a number. There has been resistance from top advisory levels of government down to the private citizen against instituting a **Universal Identifying Number** commonly called a UID, for identifying a person in all files. The Social Security number is being used as such with increasing frequency. A recent court case illustrates the concern about turning people into numbers. A man petitioned the court to have his name changed to a number and his request was denied by the judge. The judge ruled that a number was not a suitable replacement for a name!

Another complaint against our computerized society is the frequent lack of human response to problems caused by data errors or exceptions to the programmed rules. Indeed the highest level of frustration towards computers at this time arises from simple billing foul-ups which have caused months, even years, of inconvenience and unnecessary expense to consumers. They sometimes have to go to extreme measures to be listened to by someone with the authority to make the correction. It is suggested by one author that one of our "rights" in this automated age is the right to human response from any company using computer services.

Equity

The development of large computerized information networks such as the VIEW DATA system in England is being viewed with alarm. These systems could replace or drastically change newspapers, magazines, postal service, encyclopedias, libraries, consumer information and advertising. Information systems can be viewed as a source of power from several angles. First, who has access to the system to use the information, and second, who has access to the system to provide the information? In a sense, information can be viewed as a utility of the future which will need to be regulated like other public utilities to assure fair distribution of information to everyone. One of the most serious issues to be faced in the coming decade is that of **equity** in the distribution of computing knowledge and computing power. The "haves" and the "have nots" of the future will be those who have computing knowledge and power as opposed to those who do not.

At present computer technology tends to reinforce the haves or the so-called "establishment." The larger businesses have the capital needed to introduce computer technology. Once the investment is made, the resulting speed, efficiency, productivity, and power in the marketplace tend to overcome competitors who didn't have the capital to make an investment in computer technology. An example of this is the LEXIS system, a legal retrieval system designed to provide case citings to law firms. The system has been criticized because it was developed for the needs of large law firms catering to wealthy clients rather than the needs of the lower end of the legal spectrum, such as the public defender, where such a system could be of great social value. **Equity** of computer knowledge, power, and information distribution will affect every area of our lives. The ability to compete as students in the classroom, as consumers or producers in the marketplace, as defendants in the courtroom, as citizens in a democracy will all be affected.

Isolation
Another concern related to home information systems such as the VIEW DATA system mentioned above, is that of **isolation.** With computing activity centered in the home and encompassing functions that are now served out of the home, such as at libraries, stores, schools and offices, will people interact only with machines and lose much of the interaction with other people that occurs now? The isolation syndrome has already been noticed and is being studied in children who have television and computer games which they can play by themselves. These games can be just as challenging and exciting as the games played with other children, but the socialization process which goes on between children is being lost (Fig. 7.2).

In fact, arcade electronic games have been banned in the Phillipines because the country's leaders felt that they were detrimental to the youth. In the U.S.A. the Federal Aviation Administration has banned handheld electronic games on airplanes because they interfered with the navigational equipment and the beeping and buzzing disturbed other passengers.

There is the fear that we are starting to condition a generation of children who will be more comfortable relating to machines than to other people. For years there have been jokes about the weird, but brilliant, systems analysts and programmers who can only communicate with the computers they program. Many science fiction stories have also followed that theme. Perhaps these stereotypes will become a reality in the future if we are not careful to anticipate and prevent it.

Instant Democracy
It has been suggested by some that we do away with our representative government and go to a computer based "pure" democracy. Everyone could vote on the issues via computer terminals.

Figure 7.2   Will we lose our human interaction?

Whether we preserve the legislative system which we have today or go to **instant democracy** depends on our attitudes about our human legislators and the institutions of government as they exist today. There is already a growing concern by the public that politicians rely too heavily upon opinion polls to shape legislative policy. If such poll-taking becomes instantaneous and universal because everyone has a computer terminal, the potential for abuse is also increased.

ECONOMIC IMPLICATIONS

Automation

Another area of concern is the increased **automation** made possible by computers. Automation is defined by Webster as "the automatically controlled operation of an apparatus, process or system by mechanical or electronic devices that take the place of human observation, effort and decision." This carries with it the implication of replacing human labor with machine labor, and even human thinking with machine thinking.

A computer with the proper sensing devices can duplicate, and in many cases improve upon, the physical and mental capabilities of a skilled worker! In fact, automation has been said to introduce a type of "slave" labor to the labor force against which expensive human labor cannot compete for many tasks (Fig. 7.3). This slave labor never gets bored no matter how many times the task has to be repeated!

Automation has been a social concern since the onset of the Industrial Revolution in the early 1800's in Europe. However, it was not until the 1950's and 1960's that the reality of unemployment due to computer-related automation became an emotional issue in this country. At that time statements were made predicting that 50% of the work force would be disrupted by the "new wave"

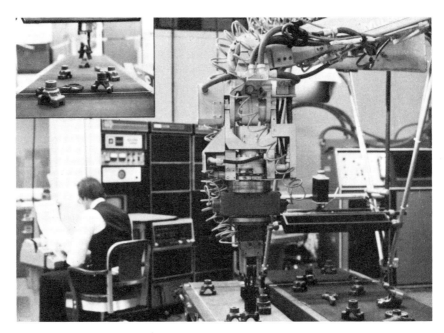

Figure 7.3   A large industrial robot equipped with vision capability which can identify and properly handle parts according to a pre-programmed scheme.

Courtesy of General Motors Corp.

of automation. The fear of massive unemployment caused by the computer revolution has not been realized, but more subtle trends can be seen. In some industries there has been much employee retraining and reassignment, rigid enforcement of retirement regulations, lack of attrition replacement, and even incentives offered for early retirement in an attempt to shrink the work force without forcing unemployment. Entry into the work force of such industries by new workers has been more difficult.

Looking at the overall employment trends during the past two decades, the relative size of the work force remains about the same with only a small increase in unemployment related to automation. There are many other factors, such as women reentering the work force, which have had a greater impact upon employment statistics. Worker productivity has increased with increasing automation, and numerous new jobs have been created by computer-related industries. Some of these new jobs require a higher level of skills, but others require lesser skills than the jobs which have been replaced by automation. In the long run, automation will probably mean shorter, more flexible working hours and more leisure for everyone. We all may have to change our attitudes toward work and leisure.

Electronic Funds Transfer

Electronic Funds Transfer Systems (EFTS) use modern computer technology combined with advanced telecommunications networks. Money is treated like any other information. When you barter or pay cash, information is transferred by exchanging objects. When you write a check or use a credit card, information is recorded on paper. When you use an EFT system, the information is recorded electronically.

The optimistic projections of an instantaneous, nationwide system have not yet materialized although many successful local systems are in operation. The typical system allows check verification and cashing at the supermarket with great speed and accuracy. The larger systems envisioned have not yet proven to be cost effective. Paper transactions have not risen in cost as was expected, but have held their own at about $.30 per transaction for nearly a decade. Credit card transactions cost about $.50 a transaction while electronic funds transfers cost as much as $1.75 each. The ultimate goal is to lower that cost to $.05 per transaction, still costly compared to cash transactions at about $.03 each!(1)

Proponents of EFTS foresee the consumer performing all essential banking transactions at remote terminals, having 24-hour access to bank services, and being provided with instant low-cost loans based on their established line of credit. However, there are many reservations about a nationwide EFTS. For one thing, the consumer would have to learn to live without the **float** — that interest-free time interval between the receipt of a check or credit card transaction and the final settling of the account. With EFTS transactions that are instantaneous the float will be eliminated. There are also serious questions regarding individual privacy in such a system. Sufficient safeguards and regulations would have to be established. The postal department is also resisting EFTS because of the impact on postal business. Now 65% of all first class mail involves financial transactions, and without this volume, postal rates would be forced to rise again.

The possibility of electronic embezzlement in a nationwide EFTS is very great. If only a tiny fraction of the programmers and technicians involved in such systems were involved in illegal schemes with the system, the cost would still be enormous. So far consumer resistance, soaring costs, legal snarls, and security and privacy risks have halted the rush to nationwide EFTS. However, as personal computing increases in the home, you can be sure that EFTS will be an issue we will have to face in the near future.

Computer Crime

A further source of economic concern in this age of computers is the computer perpetrated crime, such as that alluded to in the previous section. Typically these crimes include improper use of data files to steal or alter information contained in them, embezzle funds into phony accounts, or set up dummy corporations such as the recent Equity Funding pyramid scheme (2).

One of the most well-known of the computer frauds is the "round down" fraud involving accumulation of fractional cents. First reported in 1968 in the Wall Street Journal, this crime involved setting up a dummy account on a system where large numbers of financial accounts are regularly processed for interest. Whenever a fractional cent occurs which is equal to or larger than .5 of a cent, the cent is put into the dummy account rather than into the customer's account. Otherwise the fractional cent is dropped, as is the normal case. This fraud has a very small impact on individual customers, but can accumulate into significant sums for the dummy account over a period of time. This fraud can be detected with very careful auditing, but would slip through a routine audit since the total account sums would balance. As a matter of fact "round down" fraud has been around for years before computerized banking but has become easier to implement and hide in the complex computer programs used for banking. "How many programmers have retired to a life of leisure as their programs, long trusted and forgotten, continue to pump the pennies into their accounts at nearly the speed of light?" (4)

Computer crimes usually share three characteristics: the perpetrators get away with huge sums of money (on the average $439,000 compared to $10,000 for a typical full service bank robbery!); their crime is usually detected only by chance; and the punishment for convicted computer criminals is typically very light (3). Not only is it difficult to develop a case involving **computer crime** due to its highly technical nature, but judges tend to be very sympathetic to white collar criminals because their crimes are impersonal and nonviolent. In the famous telephone company swindle of the late 1960's, the defendant stole over $1 million worth of electronic gear from Pacific Telephone over the course of two years. He received 60 days on a prison work farm and was released in 40 days for being a model prisoner. He now makes a comfortable living by showing potential victims how to protect themselves against computer crime! (4)

Another type of computer crime being viewed with alarm by experts in the field is that perpetrated by juvenile system hackers. These are young whiz kids who delight in electronically breaking into the computer files or systems of large companies and creating havoc. Sometimes there are rings of these bandits linked up by telephone over an entire area who can do thousands of dollars of electronic vandalism at the speed of electricity. It has been suggested that society needs to channel their computer expertise into constructive projects.

Computer fraud is growing at an alarming rate—the cases that have been detected show a growth rate higher than most other types of crime. As our society converts to widespread use of electronic funds transfer, the potential for computer crime will dramatically increase to the detriment of society as a whole. The cost of the particular crime, as well as the costs incurred to prevent other such crimes, will be paid for by the consumer. In the future, stiffer sentencing by judges will be needed to discourage computer-assisted white collar crime.

The frustration level and distrust of computers by some people have resulted in another type of computer crime, "computer murders" (Fig. 7.4). There are documented cases of modern-day Luddites (Chapter 3) exhibiting violent behavior toward computers. There was a California sheriff who shot a computer for uncontrollably spewing out arrest records. Another person poured honey into newly installed terminals at the Minneapolis Post Office. A computer at an insurance company was brutally attacked by a person wielding a screwdriver. More subtle forms of sabotage also take place, such as intentionally putting bad data into a computer and blatantly refusing to use or acknowledge computer output.

Figure 7.4 Will we resort to violence against machines?

ARTIFICIAL INTELLIGENCE

Machines That Think

In the late 1960's, there was much wild speculation about the possibility of producing within a decade "intelligent" machines whose cognitive abilities would

surpass those of humans. During the ensuing years the fervor has abated due to
many problems encountered in **artificial intelligence** research; however,
machines have been programmed to do some remarkable things. They can play
Tic-Tac-Toe and Checkers with great success and Chess with reasonable success. Shakey, a famous computer-controlled robot at the Stanford Research Institute, is equipped with sensing devices enabling it to travel around the building upon command. It can seek objects, manipulate them, and devise ways to
carry out the commands if there are obstacles or heights which would prevent it
from doing so.

Intelligence is defined as the "ability to understand relationships between
facts, to discover meanings and recognize truth, to adapt to novel situations
and to learn, to improve the level of performance on the basis of past experience." **Artificial intelligence (AI)** is then defined as "the science of making
machines do what would require intelligence if done by men." Whenever we
program a machine that can understand information, adapt and improve the
strategy (such as the chess-playing programs), we have created artificial intelligence. The purpose of AI research is to duplicate the power of human reasoning in machines.

The Turing Test

Another famous test for machine intelligence was proposed by the English
mathematician, Alan Turing, in 1936. In the Turing test for intelligence, if a
human using a machine could not distinguish between human and machine
response, then the machine was regarded as "intelligent." There have been
programs such as the ELIZA question-answering program which have passed
the Turing test to a limited degree. To be truly intelligent, a machine must have
the ability to adapt to its environment and to react to totally unforeseen circumstances. Thus far, all computer applications have failed to meet such
stringent criteria.

The components necessary for artificial intelligence are memory, pattern
recognition, learning, language translation, and ability to play games. The
most overwhelming problem has proven to be programming a computer to
understand natural language due to the ambiguity and contextual differences of
natural language. Another problem is the huge number of decisions which are
possible in a problem-solving environment such as game-playing. For example,
in the game of Chess there are an estimated 10 to the 120th power possible
game paths to take in a complete Chess game. In a recent World Chess Cham-
pionship, the computer was able to consider 211,150 possible moves in 141
seconds during a typical move. When the number of paths is pruned to manage-
able size, the result is only an average chess player. One of the significant
differences between people and machines is the human ability to determine
which information is important and which is not.

Research in this area seems to be leading towards incorporating more feedback control mechanisms (i.e. "ears," "eyes," "hands") into the machine.

There is also work being done to separate tasks appropriate to people or machines according to their strengths. Humans are inventive and flexible. They are able to abstract and make associations; however they are forgetful, inaccurate, and subject to boredom. On the other hand, computers are fast, accurate and consistent, but lack flexibility. A human-machine symbiosis which capitalizes on the strength of both could prove to be a powerful team (Fig. 7.5).

Figure 7.5 A robot of the future seen at the Federal Computer Show in Washington D.C.

Photo by Rudy Potenzone

LONG-RANGE IMPACT

Much of the future impact of computers depends upon our attitudes and literacy about computers today. One trend of thought suggests that it is already too late to stem the tide: People have set in motion forces so powerful that computers will no longer be merely instrumental in shaping the future, but will be the causing agent. This group feels that we have already become so dependent on computers that it is just a matter of time before we relinquish our humanity completely.

Another school of thought believes that as long as we keep sight of those things which make us human, the computer will be an instrument for enhancing the quality of life and developing that part of ourselves which is truly human, our creativity, to undreamed of capabilities.

Robotics

As we have seen, computers are machines that are CADETS, they "Can't Add, Don't Even Try." This connotes the idea that a computer does no thinking on its own, it can only follow the strict orders of a computer program. A computer is only as smart as the programmers directing it, or is it? Currently computer scientists, mathematicians and even philosophers are attempting to create computers and computer programs that *"think."* This form of artificial intelligence will, they hope, spawn an age of computers that can "speak" and understand not only the sounds of spoken language but the meaning and nuances of language. That means computers could write stories, examine news stories for inferences and impact. It means **robots** could tirelessly perform assembly line tasks, and do things too dangerous for human beings. Robots could deal with our toxic wastes and our adventures into space. Imagine a war fought by robots, with no blood spilled in battle!

Robots equipped with artificial intelligence programs will be able to take care of many daily tasks (Fig. 7.6), the dangerous tasks and even the most skillful tasks. It may happen that robots, controlled by firemen, will go into burning buildings. Robots which wouldn't require the same life support systems as humans, could be used for space explorations. Robots will be built and programmed to perform micro eye surgery (5).

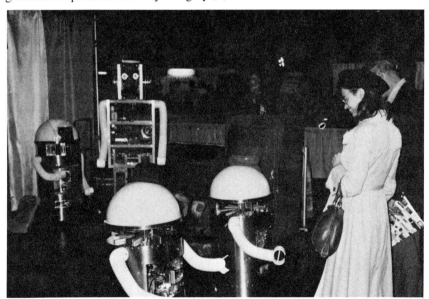

Figure 7.6   Robots designed to assist with household duties are displayed at the Federal Computer Show in Washington D.C.   *Photo by Stephen R. Heller*

As in everything, where there is a good side, there is also a sinister side to the future of computers. We have only to remind ourselves about "2001" (See

Chapter 2). There is the fear that computers will cooperate in an effort to take control! The danger exists that humans will become too dependent on the computer even for simple jobs. Futhermore, computers could become so "clever" at synthesizing information that the conclusions reached by these machines could not be understood by humans. Taken all together, the concern is that we may "program" ourselves out of existence. It has been suggested that we take care lest the computer extend its reach beyond our grasp.

Where then will the impact of computers be felt? Everywhere! Currently the CYRUS program at Yale is capable of "seeing" relationships between happenings. The program is capable of analyzing news stories about Cyrus Vance, the former Secretary of State. Having read the information, the program is asked to make inferences from the information it knows. Extending this idea, if a computer can read a book, and answer some questions on its content AND meaning, why can't that computer write its own version of the information? An impact on all journalistic areas is possible. An intelligent computer could read the newspaper and make inferences which would allow it to make "buy" or "sell" orders to a stock broker. Currently word processors abound in the office. Intelligent word processors could conduct much of the standard business of the day. According to Patrick Winston of Massachusetts Institute of Technology's articial intelligence laboratory, "in 50 years we will look back and wonder how we got along without artificial intelligence.....just as today it is beyond comprehension how we ever managed to run banks without computers doing the bookkeeping."

We have already noted the programs that can help a doctor with diagnosis, a lawyer with legal searches, a chemist with laboratory problems. Such programs would allow the paraprofessional to take on the routine work of an expert, freeing the expert for the most specialized work and allowing the expert to plot "new courses in the sky." New search systems offer us rapid retrieval of information. This is especially important in many life threatening instances when searching for data in books would be too slow. The access to computerized information retrieval has many educators worried. They are concerned that this instant response phenomena will make students and professionals lazy and will deaden curiosity. They stress that it is the duty of educators to examine the new technology and act accordingly.

Computers in the Home

The new hardware designs have made the cost and size of computers appropriate for the home. The **microcomputer** or the personal computer, can be purchased for only a few hundred dollars and is capable of sophisticated operations (Fig. 7.7). Just as a college bound senior received a typewriter as a graduation present in the past, the student of the not so distant future will carry off the microcomputer on which to prepare term papers and reports. In fact, several major Ivy League universities now issue a microcomputer to incoming Freshmen.

Figure 7.7   Former President Carter uses a home computer to compile his memoirs.

Photo by UPI.

We have already examined the games and entertainment available on microcomputers. How about the labor saving devices? It is possible to hook a personal computer to electric devices around the home and operate them from the keyboard of the computer. Imagine turning on the outdoor light without leaving the side of your computer. Computer scientists see the home of the future complete with microcomputers and computer terminals. Today, every apartment sold in a New York City condominium comes with a terminal and an access code to the SOURCE. The Warner Amex Cable Communications Inc., marketers of the QUBE two-way cable system in Columbus, Ohio, have a home microprocessor which can sense smoke in a room and send a telecommunications message to the fire department. They hope to market a microprocessor in the future which will be able to sense the climate conditions in the home and adjust the heat or air conditioning automatically. Residents of the home of the future will be able to bank, shop, cook, clean and entertain by computer.

Help for the Handicapped
The microcomputer is being adapted for use by the handicapped and could allow independent living for the handicapped (Fig. 7.8). Currently there is a bank in New England which mails its computer generated bank statements on a voice

synthesized tape to the blind share holders. This enables the blind individual to "read" a bank statement in privacy.

Figure 7.8 A computer terminal for the blind has a braille writer attached to it.

Photo by S. Heller

In a recent competition sponsored by the Tandy Corporation and the Johns Hopkins Applied Physics Laboratory entrants were invited to design microcomputer systems to help the disabled. One winning design allowed paraplegics to "type" letters and papers by depressing keys with a mouth held device. A text editor processed their paperwork. Another design used the microcomputer graphics capability to teach lip reading (Fig. 7.9). Words were "mouthed" by a pair of lips which appeared on the monitor and the word being "said" was printed underneath the mouth.

The Ultimate Challenge

Potentially the most damaging impact of computers on society may prove to be the most subtle. How will people's view of themselves change in the future (Fig. 7.10)? It has been pointed out by many that this self-image has suffered three traumas in history. The first one was when Copernicus discovered that the earth was not the center of the universe. The second came when Darwin theorized the link between humans and animals. The third was when Freud suggested that people are not in control of most of their psychological make-up, but rather their subconscious is. The three blows to human ego have been cosmic, biological and psychological.

∧ **Figure 7.9**   A computer system used to aid the deaf to learn lip reading.

Photo by S. Heller

Will we now suffer a fourth blow to our self-image by removing the distinction between people and machines (6)? As we produce machines that can do more and more of the human function, will we start to view ourselves as merely the ultimate machine - "is the human brain just a computer that happens to be made out of meat?" Or even worse, will we view ourselves as an inferior machine? Or will we be able to maintain the soulish part of our being, in spite of the analogies which can be drawn between humans and machines? This may prove to be the ultimate challenge to humanity.

KEY IDEAS
Privacy
Automation
Computer Crime
Artificial Intelligence
Depersonalization
Equity
Isolation
Electronic Funds Transfer System
Universal Identifying Number
Robot
Microcomputer

Figure 7.10   Will our view of ourselves change?

ACTIVITIES

Your Number Please

Plan a "numbers only" day when everyone in your class or school is assigned an ID card with a number. You won't be able to do anything that day without your number. You won't be able to eat lunch, go to recess, go to the library to get a book, etc. If you lose your number, you will have to find a way to get a new one. The next day, talk about how you felt being "only a number."

TEACHER'S CORNER

Purpose: To increase the student's understanding of the role that identification numbers play in our society.

Materials: Index cards or mimeographed ID cards upon which the mock ID numbers are recorded, markers.

Time: One day.
Skills: Communication.
Additional Information: The activities in this section could be assigned on a selective basis to individuals or teams who would then report back to the class. All of the issues presented in this section are important and could be presented individually throughout the year or as a unit on social concern.

Not Computer Goofs

1. Collect articles for a class bulletin board which are about computer "mistakes." Be ready to discuss whether the computer or the people using the computer made the mistake.

2. Write a class skit which shows how people sometimes blame computers for mistakes. In your skit show how most of these mistakes are made by people. For example: A clerk enters $200 on your charge account instead of $20. You receive a bill from the computer for $200 and you call the store. You are told it is a computer mistake. Is it really?

3. Describe ways in which people might be affected if a large computer system, such as a banking system, failed due to an electrical or mechanical failure.

TEACHER'S CORNER

Purpose: To increase the students' awareness of what is and what is not a computer mistake.
Materials: Recent newspapers, magazines.
Time: Ongoing project.
Skills: Thinking, reading comprehension, written expression, verbal expression.
Additional Information: This could be part of a larger unit on consumer education and advertising.

Filed Away

Interview an adult to find out all of the data files that contain information about that person: for example, social security, census, internal revenue, motor vehicle, library...etc.

TEACHER'S CORNER

Purpose: To increase the student's awareness of the proliferation of data files in our society and the possible impact on the privacy of an individual.
Materials: Teacher created worksheet.
Time: Homework assignment.
Skills: Written expression, verbal expression.

Do's and Don'ts

Make up a set of rules which you think should control the use of any data bank with personal information in it. For example, you might include: Who can use the information? Who can change the information? Present these rules to the class for discussion.

TEACHER'S CORNER
Purpose: To increase the student's awareness of data banks and the ethical issues related to them.
Materials: Paper, pencil, pen.
Time: 30 minutes.
Skills: Thinking, written expression, verbal expression, research.

Instant Democracy

Plan a day when every action the class takes must be voted upon. Be prepared for a difficult day. When you have finished the "instant democracy," talk about what happened. Do computers make "instant democracy" possible?

TEACHER'S CORNER
Purpose: To provide the experience of "instant democracy" to the students as a springboard for discussing the use of computers for opinion polls.
Materials: A ballot box and ballots for voting.
Time: One day.
Skills: Communication.
Additional Information: The class may devise a clever way to accomplish the voting.

That's Debatable

Plan a debate about a checkless/cashless society. Have one team argue for all the positive things about this issue. Have the other team present all the negative aspects.

TEACHER'S CORNER
Purpose: To provide discussion about the impact of electronic funds transfer systems on our society.
Materials: Tables, chairs organized for a debate, books that have information about electronic funds transfer (see Related Readings).
Skills: Verbal expression, persuasion, organization.
Additional Information: Your local banking associations might offer some information about electronic funds transfer.

Twenty Questions

Develop a questionnaire to find out information about another person. Team up with classmates to "answer" each other's questions. You are to answer only those questions you want to and leave the others blank. Afterwards, you can discuss why you didn't answer certain questions. Examples of questions might be: What is your name? Where do you live? How much money do you have in the bank? Who is your favorite teacher?

TEACHER'S CORNER
Purpose: To give students the opportunity to think about the concept of privacy as it relates to themselves.
Materials: Paper, pencil.
Time: 30-60 minutes.
Skills: Written expression, verbal expression.

Legal Beagles
Look up articles or ask a lawyer about the laws that have been enacted relating to computers. Hint: Look up the Freedom of Information Act of 1966-1967, the Fair Credit Reporting Act of 1970, the Privacy Act of 1974, or a computer crime law which may have been enacted by your state. (See California, in particular)

TEACHER'S CORNER
Purpose: To provide students with a view of how computers have changed our legal system.
Materials: Library reference books.
Time: One-week report.
Skills: Research, written expression, oral expression.

Only the Lonely
Write a story about a person who does all activities by computer: shopping, school, library, voting, and working. You might imagine what it would be like to communicate with a machine most of the time instead of communicating with people.

TEACHER'S CORNER
Purpose: To provide a vehicle for students to increase their awareness of the isolation which can be increased by computers in our society.
Materials: Paper, pencil.
Time: One hour.
Skills: Creativity, written expression.

What Do You Think?
Discuss the things that make a human intelligent. What do animals do that make them seem intelligent? What can machines do that make them seem intelligent?

TEACHER'S CORNER
Purpose: To make the students think about the issue of artificial intelligence.
Materials: Pencil and paper, chalkboard and chalk.

Time: 15-30 minutes.
Skills: Verbal expression.
Additional Information: The teacher could lead this discussion as a "brainstorming" session in which all of the ideas are written on the board as they come and are organized afterwards.

A Day in Court

Set up a courtroom to put PRIVACY on trial. Do we or do we not have the right to privacy? Use witnesses for and against privacy, and a jury to decide the fate of privacy.

TEACHER'S CORNER
Purpose: To help students develop an awareness of society's need for information versus the individual's right to privacy.
Materials: Classroom set-up for a trial, like a courtroom.
Time: One week to prepare, 45 minutes to an hour to present.
Skills: Verbal expression, organization, research.

Is It a Crime?

Take the time to talk about what is 'Computer Crime'. You might want to include some of these questions in your discussion.

1. Is it a crime to run your personal programs on a company computer?
2. Is it a crime to give your class account on the computer to a friend?
3. Is it a crime to give a friend a copy of a program for his homework?
4. Is it a crime to break a code to find out secret or personal information just for fun?
5. Is it a crime to give that information away?
6. Is it a crime to transfer money from one bank account to another, even if you will pay it back soon?
7. Is it a crime to write a program you know has some mistakes in it, but not tell anyone?

TEACHER'S CORNER
Purpose: To raise the ethical questions of using the computer to commit crimes.
Materials: Teacher created worksheet.
Time: 30-60 minutes.
Skills: Verbal expression.

Rip Van Twinky in The 21st Century

Read aloud and act out the following play in class. Give your opinion about the situations created in the play.

TEACHER'S CORNER
Purpose: This play provides a springboard for discussion of the social impact of computers.
Materials: 8 copies of the play for 7 speaking parts and the teacher.
Time: 8 minutes for the play, 15-20 minutes for discussion.
Skills: Reading, role playing, verbal.
Additional Information: It is suggested that the teacher use a vocabulary list with this play. The words used are:

automation
data bank
privacy
artificial intelligence
electronic funds transfer
instant democracy
depersonalization
isolation
universal identification number

These could be put on the blackboard or on a mimeographed sheet for the student. Since there are seven speaking parts in the play, the teacher could involve other students in this activity by having them look up the words in a dictionary. After the play is read, the students who looked up the words will give their definitions. The teacher will need to guide the discussion so that the students see the parallel between the vocabulary words and the ideas in the play.

This play could be presented as a class project. See "Do It Yourself Computer" for making props. Although there are only seven speaking parts, the whole class could participate in the computer scene.

A number of books written about computers and society during the past 10 years provide a good source for opinions on the issues. See the Chapter 7 "Related Readings" section for a list of such books is included. Any one of these books would be sufficient reference for use as background information on the issues.

RIP VAN TWINKY IN THE 21ST CENTURY

The scene opens in the present with our star, Rip Van Twinky, bragging to his friend Joe about his new computer.

RIP: With my new computer I'll be able to find the answers for all of my math homework problems. I can use it to write my English compositions, too. I won't have to bother with boring math facts or spelling or learning history dates ever again.

JOE: But Rip, if you let the computer do all of your homework for you, you won't learn anything yourself.

RIP: So what! Pretty soon computers will do everything for us. I've heard that our money will be replaced by electronic funds transfer - our books and magazines will be put on computer - best of all, our teachers will be replaced by computers, too! Why should I knock myself out learning anything? I'll let the computer do it for me!

JOE: Well, I don't know, Rip. I think I better go home and do my homework. See you at school tomorrow.

RIP: So long, Joe. (muttering to himself) What a drag. Guess I'll play Star Trek on my computer for a while.

(RIP soon gets drowsy and falls asleep over his computer keyboard. As he sleeps, the room around him changes into a room filled with fantastic machines which speak to Rip in electronic voices.)

IQ: Wake-up. Wake-up. It is 9AM. The star date is month 5, day 11, year 2081, planet Earth.

RIP: (waking up suddenly) Where am I? Who are you?

IQ: You are in your living module. I am IQ, your personal computer. How may I assist you?

RIP: Oh, my head. I feel like I slept for 100 years. Say, what year did you say it was?

IQ: It is the year 2081.

RIP: Wow! I did sleep for 100 years. Hey, where can I get a newspaper or book to find out what it's like now?

IQ: There are no newspapers or books. They became obsolete in the year 2020. You can use the QT data terminal to find the answers to your questions.

(RIP turns on the QT data terminal.)

QT: How may I inform you?

RIP: Tell me about the year 2081. What is it like?

QT: The year 2081 is the 80th year of the computer. Humanoids are assigned an ID number and a living module at birth. They are cared for by computerized nurses until they are old enough to be educated by computer terminals. For those humanoids desiring to marry, a perfect mate is selected for them by a computer. They are assigned a job to be done from their living module by remote terminal. All money earned and spent is recorded in the central data bank. When a humanoid becomes defective, er... sick, a computerized doctor diagnoses the problem and gives the prescription. Since all manual work is now done automatically by computers, there is plenty of time to play computer games, watch computerized video screens, and listen to computer music. All decisions of government are made daily by computerized opinion polls. Thus, we have achieved instant democracy.

RIP: Wow! A real computer paradise! Tell me, IQ, how can I get in touch with my friend Joe?

IQ: That does not compute. You may contact other humanoids by computerphone if you know their ID number.

RIP: I don't know his ID, only his name.

IQ: Names are obsolete. Humanoids are assigned an ID number at birth.

RIP: (somewhat dejected) Oh. Say, I'm hungry. How do I get something to eat?

IQ: Activate the food intake computer, I.C.U.R Hungry. Then program your intake choice.

RIP: Let's see. Which one is that? This must be it. (Rip turns on the I.C.U.R.)

I.C.U.R.: I.C.U.R. Hungry, at your service.

RIP: I'd like a Big Mcburger, a milkshake, and some french fries.

I.C.U.R.: That does not compute. Input number of calories desired.

RIP: Uh, 950.

I.C.U.R: Input desired protein, carbohydrates, and fats in grams.

RIP: Hmmm, how about 20, 10, and 5. Now do I get my Big Mcburger?

I.C.U.R.: That does not compute. (I.C.U.R dispenses a large green pill and a glass of water.) Here is your intake pill to be taken with 50 ml of water.

RIP: Yuck! IQ, is there any other way to get real food around here?

IQ: You can order merchandise through the TZ-90 shopping terminal over there.

(Rip turns on the terminal.)

TZ-90: What is your ID number?

RIP: Uh, my name is Rip Van Twinky. I'd like to order some food.

TZ-90: That does not compute. I must have your ID number in order to charge your purchase to your account.

RIP: Oh, that's not necessary. I have enough money to pay for my Big McBurger in cash.

TZ-90: That does not compute. Cash became obsolete in 1990. All money is now in the computer as electronic funds. Repeat, what is your ID number?

RIP: I just got here - I don't have an ID number.

TZ-90: All humanoids are given an ID at birth. Security! Red alert! Security!

SECURITY: What's the problem?

TZ-90: This humanoid claims that it does not have an ID number.

SECURITY: I will check my data banks. What is your identification?

RIP: Rip Van Twinky.

SECURITY: Date of birth?

RIP: June 11, 1968. I'm 13 years old.

SECURITY: That does not compute! You are not in my data banks. Therefore you do not exist. You cannot buy anything. You cannot be educated. You cannot vote. You cannot read the data terminals. You do not exist!

(Machines start to surround RIP clamoring "disconnect unit," "invalid data," "that does not compute" and then they fade into the distance.)

MOM: Rip! Wakeup! It's time for dinner and you haven't finished your homework.

RIP: (wakes up with a start) Please, Mom, no more green pills.

MOM: What are you talking about? What green pills? You must have been dreaming.

RIP: Phew! You mean I can eat real food and read real books and spend real money?

MOM: Of course you can, you silly boy. Now wash up for dinner. (Mom leaves the room.)

RIP: What a relief! I guess I'd better do my homework after all. I'm not ready for computers to do everything for me yet!

Rip turns off his computer terminal and leaves the room.

RELATED READINGS

(**S** -Student, **T** -Teacher)
1. Adams, J. Mack, Haden, Douglas. *Social Effects of Computer Use and Misuse*. John Wiley & Sons, 1970. (**T**)
2. Arbib, Michael. *Computers in Cybernetic Society*. Academic Press, 1977. (**T**)
3. Benquai, August. *Computer Crime*. D.C. Heath & Company, 1978. (**T**)
4. Brown, John. *Computers and Automation*. ARCO Publishing Company, 1968. (**S,T**)
5. Deken, Joseph. *The Electronic Cottage*. William Morrow, 1981. (**T**)
6. Evans, Christopher. *Micro Millenium*. Viking Press, Inc., 1980. (**T**)
7. Levy, David. *Chess and Computers*. Computer Science Press, 1976. (**T**)
8. Levy, David, Newborn, Monroe. *More Chess and Computers*. Computer Science Press, 1980. (**T**)
9. Logsdon, Tom. *Computers and Social Controversy*. Computer Science Press, 1980. (**T**)
10. Mowshowitz, Abbe. *The Conquest of Will: Information Processing in Human Affairs*. Addison Wesley Publishing Co., 1976. (**T**)
11. Parker, Donn. *Crime By Computer*. Charles Scribner's Sons, 1976. (**T**)
12. Rothman, Stanley, Mosemann, Charles. *Computers and Society*. Science Research Associates, 1976. (**T**)
13. Sanders, Donald. *Computers and Society*. McGraw-Hill Book Company, 1973. (**T**)
14. Silver, Gerald. *The Social Impact of Computers*. Harcourt Brace Jovanovich, 1979. (**T**)
15. Smith, Robert Ellis. *Privacy, How to Protect What's Left of It*. Anchor Press/Doubleday, 1979. (**T**)
16. Weizenbaum, Joseph. *Computer Power and Human Reason*. W.H.Freeman & Company, 1976. (**T**)
17. Wessel, Milton. *Freedom's Edge: The Computer Threat to Society*. Addison-Wesley Publishing company, 1974. (**T**)

18. Wicklein, John. *Electronic Nightmare, The New Communications and Freedom.* The Viking Press, 1981. (**T**)
19. *IBM's Guidelines to Employee Privacy: An Interview with Frank T. Cary.* Harvard Business Review, September-October 1976. (**T**)

REFERENCES

(1) Rose, Sanford. "Checkless Banking is Bound to Come." *Fortune,* June 1977.
(2) Parker, Donn. *Crime By Computer.* Charles Scribner's Sons, 1976, Chapter 13.
(3) Logsdon, Tom. *Computers and Social Controversy.* Computer Science Press, 1980.
(4) Parker, Donn. *Crime By Computer.* Charles Scribner's Sons, 1976, Chapter 8.
(5) Stockton, William. "Creating Computers to Think Like Humans." *The New York Times Magazine,* December 7, 1980.
(6) Mazlish, Bruce. "The Fourth Discontinuity." *Technology and Culture.* January 8, 1967.

Appendix

SOFTWARE EVALUATION

With the advent of computers in the classroom, many teachers are faced with the task of deciding from many different types of commercially available, educational software. This Appendix presents two tools to aid the teacher in evaluating such software. The first, shown in Table A, is a checklist of items to be considered when reviewing an educational software package. Table B is a form on which notes can be made when reviewing a particular computer program. These two tools, for use by the teacher when previewing software packages, form a reference notebook of evaluated material.

Table A
SOFTWARE EVALUATION CHECKLIST

Purpose of the material is
    well defined
    achieved

Content of the material is
    described
    accurate
    educational
    free of stereotypes

Presentation of the material is
    in correct English sentences
    clear, logical
    appropriate level of difficulty
    with sound, color, graphics

motivational
challenging
with effective feedback
learner controlled
integrated with prior experiences
generalizable
comprehensive support materials
easy to use
using computer capabilities
normally reliable

Table B
PROGRAM LOG SHEET

Name of Program:

Company:

Brief Description:

Age Level:

Special Characteristics:(i.e., especially cute; good graphics; particularly challenging for bright students; geared to slow learners, appropriate language model used.)

Personal Reaction: (Is the program worthwhile? Would it fit in your classroom? Could this be used in your classroom if it were modified? How?)

Additional supplies needed with the program.

GENERAL TEACHING RESOURCES

1. *AEDS Journal.* Fall 1979. Association of Educational Data Systems, Washington, D.C.
2. Educational Products Information Exchange (EPIE). Stoneybrook, New York.
3. *Guidelines for Evaluating Computerized Instructional Materials.* National Council of Teachers of Mathematics, Reston, Virginia.
4. *Microcomputers in Education.* QUEUE. Fairfield, Connecticut.
5. Microcomputer Resource Center. Teachers College, Columbia University, New York, New York.
6. *MicroSIFT.* Northwest Regional Educational Laboratory, Portland, Oregon.
7. *School Microware Reviews.* Dresden Associates, Dresden, Maine.

Glossary

ABACUS: An early computing device which consisted of a frame with beads used for counting and performing arithmetic operations.

ACCESS TIME: Average amount of time required to retrieve a quantity from storage location.

ACCUMULATOR: A high speed, low capacity storage register where calculations take place in the arithmetic unit of the computer.

ADDRESS: The numbered location of a unit of memory.

ALGORITHM: A well-defined mathematical or logical solution of a problem in a finite number of steps.

ARITHMETIC UNIT: The part of the computer in which all arithmetic operations (addition, subtraction, multiplication, and division) are performed with the result being temporarily stored in the accumulator.

ARTIFICIAL INTELLIGENCE: The science of making machines do what would require intelligence if done by humans.

ASSEMBLY LANGUAGE: A programming language comprised of easy to remember codes which control the most primitive actions of the computer.

AUTOMATION: The operation or control of a process, equipment or system without human intervention.

AUXILIARY STORAGE: A storage device accessible to the computer processing circuits used to supplement the primary storage.

BASIC: (Beginners All-purpose Symbolic Instruction Code) a simple programming language.

BINARY: A number system whose base is 2 (therefore the only symbols are 0 and 1). A number system designed for electronic computers which only have two states, on and off.

BIT: (Binary digIT) smallest unit of information recognized by the computer.

BUFFER: A high speed, low capacity storage register used when data is transfered from one storage area to another.

BUG: A mistake.

BYTE: A sequence of bits acted on as a unit.

CALCULATOR: A mechanical or electronic device used to perform arithmetic operations.

CAPACITY: Amount of data that can be stored in a computer storage system, related to the size of memory.

CATHODE RAY TUBE (CRT) TERMINAL: Television-like picture tube and a keyboard used as a visual display terminal (VDT) on which images are produced. A CRT allows information to be accessed or displayed on the screen.

CENTRAL PROCESSING UNIT (CPU): The "heart" of a general purpose computer which controls interpretation and execution of instructions, input and output.

CHARACTER: Any symbol, digit, letter or special mark processed by a digital computer.

CHIPS: Microprocessors that are complex computers on a single piece of silicon.

COBOL (COmmon Business Oriented Language): A high level programming language suited to business data processing.

CODE SYSTEM: A number system based on many different symbols to represent specific quantities.

COMMAND: A signal or group of signals that cause a computer to perform one operation.

COMPATABILITY: Similar characteristics of different data processing equipment which allows one machine to interface with another.

COMPILER: A program which converts or translates a high-level language program such as FORTRAN into the machine language of the particular computer being used.

COMPUTER: A person or device which performs computations.

COMPUTER ARCHITECT: A person who designs the layout of the circuitry and electronic components of a computer.

COMPUTER ASSISTED DISPATCH SYSTEM (CADS):   An interactive computer system used by police and fire departments for allocating and dispatching emergency equipment when needed.

COMPUTER ASSISTED INSTRUCTION (CAI):   The use of computers to interact with students in the instructional process, such as with drill and practice, exercises, testing, or presenting new topics.

COMPUTER CRIME: Any crime in which the knowledge of computers is necessary for its perpetration, investigation or prosecution; also any crime in which the computer is used or abused with malicious intent.

COMPUTER GRAPHICS: The use of computer technology to process and produce pictorial data.

COMPUTER LITERATE: The state of having sufficient knowledge about computers to use them, to understand the social impact, and to know the many ways in which they are used by others.

COMPUTER MAINTENANCE ENGINEER: A person who tests and repairs the physical equipment of a computer system.

COMPUTER MANAGED INSTRUCTION (CMI):   The use of computers to aid in managing the instructional sequence, but not necessarily in instruction itself. Such a system typically is used to test student performance and in some cases, prescribe units of study for individual students.

COMPUTER OPERATOR: A person who operates the physical equipment of a computer system.

CONSULTANT: A person with specialized expertise who is called in to help analyze and solve a problem.

COURSEWARE: Computer programs written especially for educational applications.

DATA: Coded information.

DATA BANK: A comprehensive collection of libraries of data.

DATA BASE: A collection of data fundamental to a system.

DATA ENTRY CLERK: A person who is responsible for typing data which goes directly into a computer system.

DEBUGGING: The detection, location and removal of mistakes from a computer program.

DEPERSONALIZATION: The state of being without privacy or without individuality.

DIGITAL COMPUTER: A computer whose processing functions are based on counting discrete entities rather than continuous items as in an analog computer.

DIRECT ACCESS DEVICE: A computer storage device which allows either random access or semi-random access to the data values in the storage.

DISK: A flat circular plate with a magnetic surface on which data can be stored by magnetizing portions of the plate.

DISTRIBUTED PROCESSING: The concept of placing part of the computer's power and storage at various locations, where the data is generated or where the computer results are needed for effective management.

DOCUMENTATION: All of the information which describes how a program or set of programs work. It usually includes such items as an algorithm or flowchart, input and output description, and a statement of the problem being solved.

DOWNTIME: Any time interval during which a computer system is inoperative.

ELECTRONIC DATA PROCESSING (EDP): An all inclusive term referring to the overall science of converting data by electronic means into any desired form.

ELECTRONIC FUNDS TRANSFER SYSTEM (EFTS): A computerized system which allows financial transactions to take place electronically rather than on paper as with cash or checks.

EQUITY: The state of being just, impartial and fair.

EXECUTE: To run a program on the computer resulting in the output of information.

FILE: A collection of related records treated as a unit.

FILE MAINTENANCE: The processing of information in a file to keep it up to date.

FLOAT: A financial term which has to do with an interest-free period of time between a debit and a deposit caused by the time lag inherent in processing the transactions.

FLOPPY DISK: A small inexpensive magnetic disk unit in which the individual platters are made of vinyl plastic. The self lubricating properties permit constant physical contact between the recording heads and the surface of the disk.

FLOWCHART: A sketch made up of boxes of various shapes connected by arrows which portrays the structure of a computer program.

FORMAT: A predetermined arrangement of information usually in a file.

FORTRAN (FORmula TRANslation):   A symbolic computer programming language used primarily for scientific application because the expressions resemble algebraic expressions.

GARBAGE: Unwanted or meaningless information stored within a computer file.

GARBAGE IN, GARBAGE OUT (GIGO): A computer term meaning that the results (output) from a computer are only as good as the program and data entered (input).

HARD COPY: A readable machine output on paper.

HARDWARE: The physical equipment in a data processing center or computer system.

INFORMATION RETRIEVAL: Methods used in recovering specific information from computer storage.

INFORMATION STORAGE AND RETRIEVAL: A computer system which allows data to be saved and recalled according to specific parameters.

INPUT DEVICE: A device used to communicate information to the computer, such as a card reader, terminal or an optical scanning device.

INPUT-OUTPUT DEVICE: A piece of computer hardware used to achieve communication between man and computer.

INTEGRATED CIRCUIT: A combination of interconnected circuitry elements, usually highly compact, inseparably imprinted on a continuous layer of material.

INTERACTIVE: A computer system which provides immediate response and allows immediate reaction by the person using the system.

ISOLATION: The state of being separated or set apart from others.

KEYPUNCH MACHINE: A keyboard device which punches holes in a set of cardboard cards.

KEYWORD: A significant or informative word in a title or document that describes its content.

LOAD: The action of placing a program or data into the memory of a computer.

LOGO: A powerful, but simple to use, programming language developed at Massachusetts Institute of Technology for the purpose of teaching young children how to program.

LOOP: To repeat, automatically under program control, the same sequence of steps until a predetermined stop or condition occurs.

MACHINE LANGUAGE: A code, usually in binary digits, used to directly operate the computer.

MAGNETIC INK CHARACTER RECOGNITION (MICR):   A method of storing information in characters printed with ink containing particles of magnetic material. The information can be read into a computer at high speed by automatic devices.

MANAGEMENT INFORMATION SYSTEM (MIS):   A computerized information system which provides business management with data to assist in decision-making.

MAINFRAME: The central processor of a computer system containing main storage, arithmetic unit and special registers.

MEMORY: The part of a computer where information and programs are stored and manipulated.

MENU: A list of possible operator actions supplied by the software system for selection.

MICROCOMPUTER: A small, self-contained digital computer whose mainframe is made of integrated circuits.

MICROPROCESSOR: An integrated circuit component that contains the logic of a complete central processing unit.

MICROSECOND: One millionth of a second; also, how far an electron can travel in one microsecond.

MODEM: An electronic device which converts data into a form which can be transmitted over a data phone line.

MULTIPROGRAMMING: A technique for handling two or more independent programs simultaneously.

NANOSECOND: One billionth of a second; also, how far an electron can travel in one billionth of a second.

NETWORKING: Hooking together geographically separated computers over transmission lines, thus allowing them to communicate data and programs to each other.

NUMBER SYSTEM: The method used to represent quantities by a system.

OFFLINE: Equipment not under the control of the CPU.

ON-LINE: Equipment which is under the control of the CPU, and has the ability to interact with the computer, usually by a terminal.

OPERATING SYSTEM: An integrated collection of computer programs that reside in the computer and control the selection, movement, and processing of programs and data needed to solve problems.

OUTPUT DEVICE: A device used to present information from within the computer memory to the user, such as a printer or a screen.

PICOSECOND: One thousandth of a nanosecond, one trillionth of a second.

PLACE VALUE SYSTEM: A number system based on grouping quantities in relation to a particular value, such as 10 or 2, and using digits to represent groups of that value.

POINT-OF-SALE MARKETING: A technique for directly entering data into a computer system at the time the article is sold, usually by using an optical scanner/reader or magnetic scanner.

PRIMARY CIRCUITS: The main memory unit of a digital computer.

PRINTED CIRCUITS: Electronic circuits printed or vacuum deposited on thin, insulating sheets.

PRIVACY: The right of individuals to select the time and circumstances when information about them is to be discussed.

PROBLEM ORIENTED LANGUAGE: A high-level programming language such as BASIC, FORTRAN, COBOL, or **Pascal,** comprised of instructions which are related to the problem being solved rather than the computer being used. Such a language has to be compiled into the machine language of the particular computer being used.

PROCESSOR: A computer capable of receiving data, manipulating it and supplying results.

PROGRAM: A set of instructions arranged for directing digital computers to perform desired operations.

PROGRAMMER: A person who designs and codes programs to solve problems using a computer.

PROGRAMMER, BUSINESS: A person who investigates and analyzes business systems within a company for possible conversion to electronic processing and who develops the computer programs and associated documentation necessary to implement such systems.

PROGRAMMER, SCIENTIFIC: A person who uses computers in ways that are classified as non-business and relate to various scientific or research problem-solving questions or programs. Such programs are characterized by relatively low volumes of input, processing, and output.

PROGRAMMER, SYSTEMS: A person who designs and writes programs which are used by computers to control the flow of operations of a computer system.

PROGRAMMING LANGUAGE: Any well-defined language used in preparing instructions for computer execution.

PUNCHED CARD: A card punched with a pattern of holes to represent data.

RANDOM ACCESS DEVICE: Any computer storage device in which the time required to retrieve a particular data value is not significantly affected by its physical location, similar to finding a song on a record.

READ ONLY MEMORY (ROM):   A memory in which the information is stored at the time of manufacture. This information can only be modified with great difficulty.

RECORD: A collection of related data treated as a unit.

REAL-TIME PROCESSING: A data processing operation in which the results of the process being monitored are received so quickly they can be used to influence the continuing operation of the process.

REGISTER: A device that can contain a computer word, character or portion of a word. The register holds information for manipulation.

REMOTE TERMINAL: An array of input-output devices connected to a distant computer by means of telephone lines or other telecommunication channels.

ROBOT: Any machine or device which is programmed to automatically perform some function.

SAND GROOVE: An early computational device in which pebbles were put in grooves in the sand to record the amount of a transaction.

SEMICONDUCTOR: A substance, such as selenium, which usually insulates against the flow of electricity but which under special conditions can be made to conduct electricity.

SEQUENTIAL ACCESS DEVICE: A computer storage unit in which a stored quantity can be retrieved only by passing through other information, similar to finding a song on a cassette tape.

SIMULATION: The representation of a system or process by a symbolic (usually mathematical) model.

SOFTWARE: Programs including systems, library routines, and other service programs that govern the operation of a computer.

SOFTWARE PROJECT MANAGER: A person who directs the activities of a group of systems analysts and programmers working together to write a system of programs for a particular application.

SORT: To arrange data in an ordered sequence.

STORAGE: Computer oriented medium in which data is contained.

STORED PROGRAM COMPUTER: A digital computer that stores instructions in memory which can be programmed to change its own instructions and execute them in their changed form.

SYSTEMS ANALYST: A person who studies the overall operation and flow of information through an environment and helps to plan how the computer could be utilized in that environment.

TABULATOR: A device used to accumulate totals based on the data coded on punched cards.

TALLY STICK: A device used by the early Romans for recording a business transaction; horizontal marks were made to denote the amount and the stick would then be split vertically so that each party had a record of the transaction.

TALLY SYSTEM: A number system based on repeating a few symbols as many times as is required to represent a particular quantity.

TERMINAL: A point in a system where the data can be entered or received.

TIME SHARING: Occurs when a computer's time is sequentially apportioned among several different users. The response time is so short that each user seems to have a dedicated computer.

TRANSISTOR: A three terminal semiconductor device used for amplification or switching.

UNIVERSAL IDENTIFICATION NUMBER (UID):   A number which would be necessary for identifying an individual in a computerized society.

USER: A person who uses or interacts in some way with a computer or computer system.

VACUUM TUBE: An electron tube having an internal vacuum sufficiently high to permit electrons to move with low interactions, reducing the amount of heat produced.

VARIABLE: A symbol or mnemonic given within a computer program representing a location that may change in value during the execution of that program.

VIDEO-DISPLAY TERMINAL (VDT):   A display screen that allows keyed or stored information to be viewed for reading or editing.

WORD: One unit of addressable memory used to store an instruction or piece of data.

WORD PROCESSING: Transition of written, verbal or recorded word to verbal, typewritten or printed form through a storage medium that allows information to be manipulated before it is committed to final form.

Index

171